THIS BOOK BELONGS TO:

____

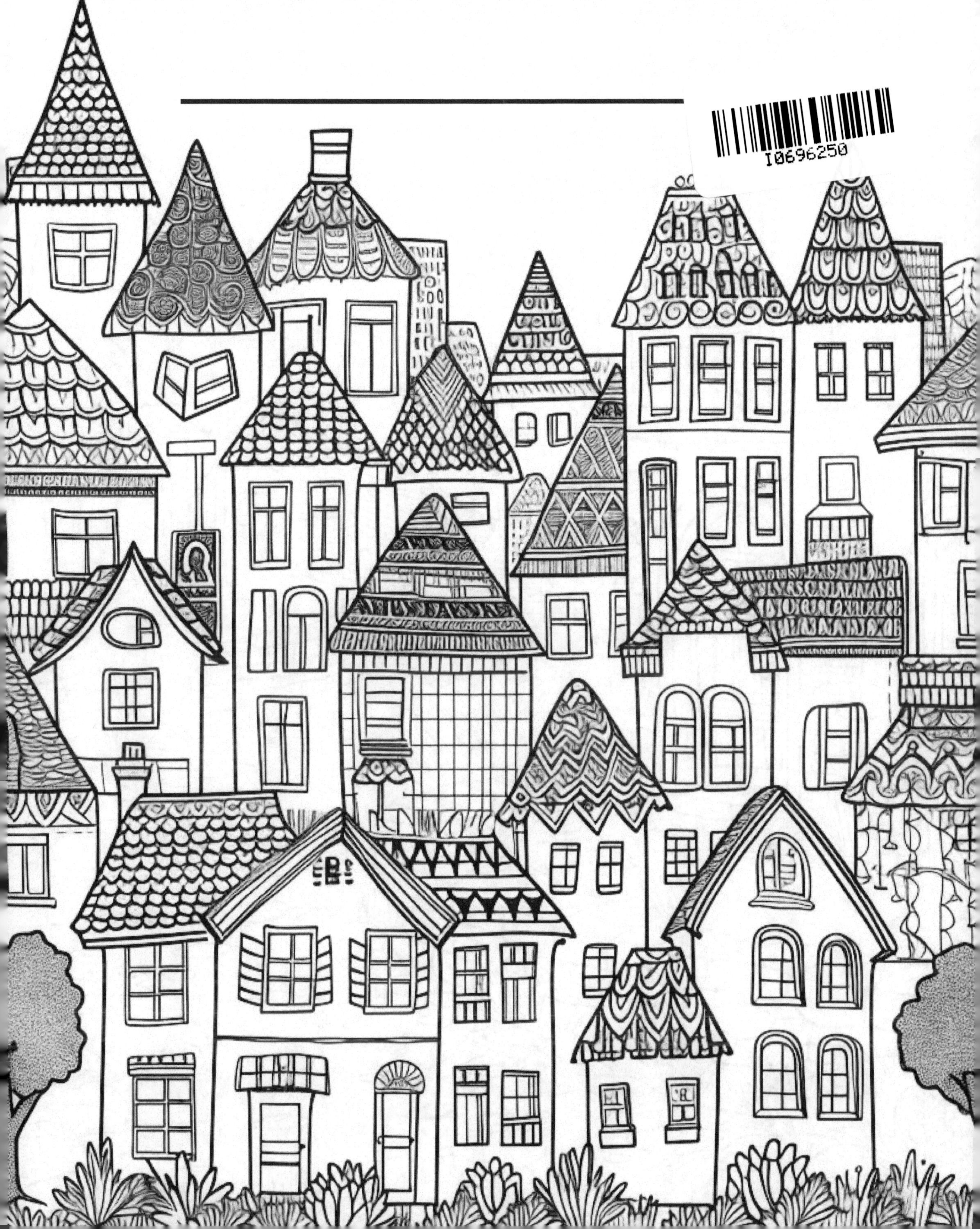

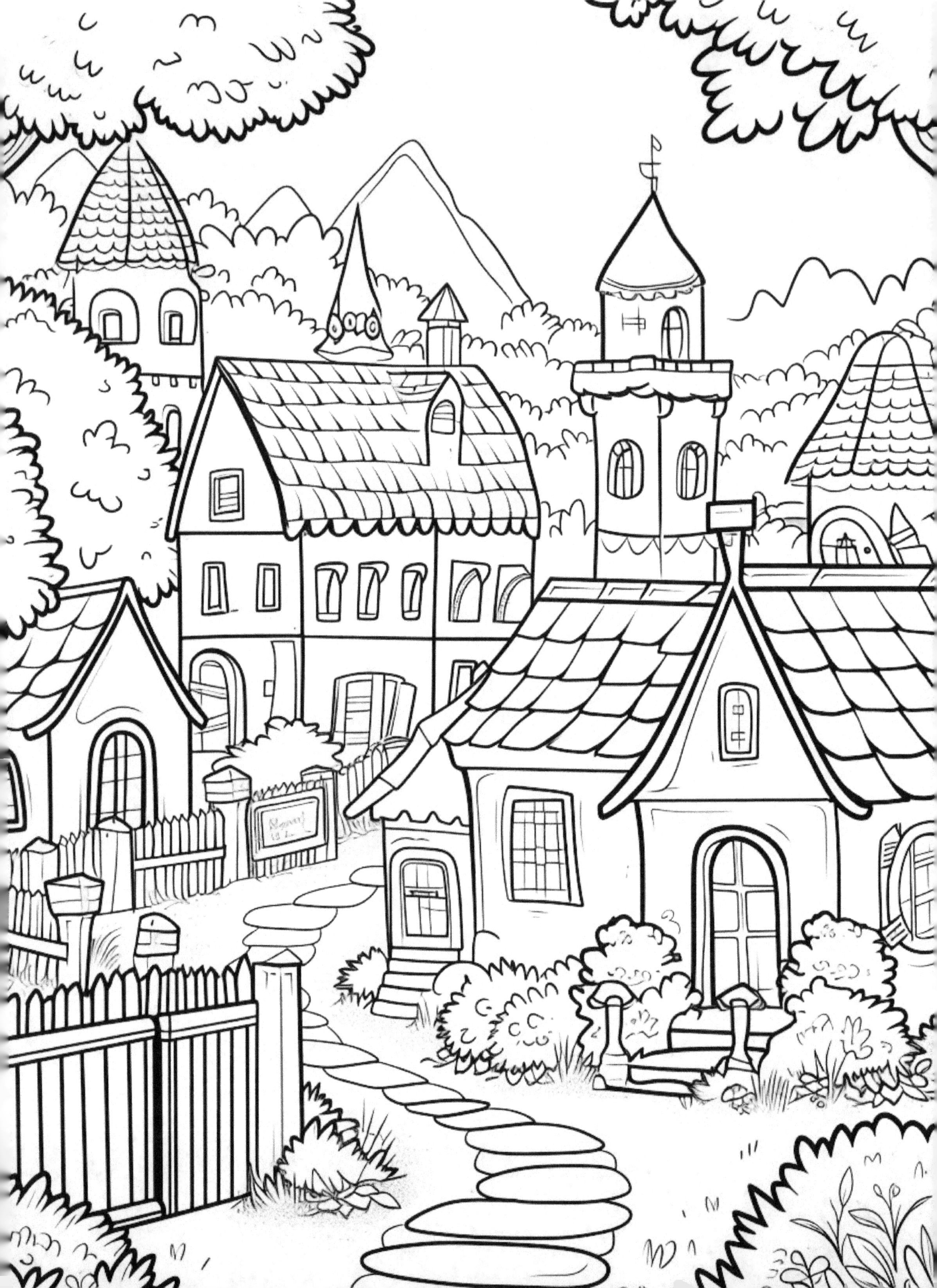

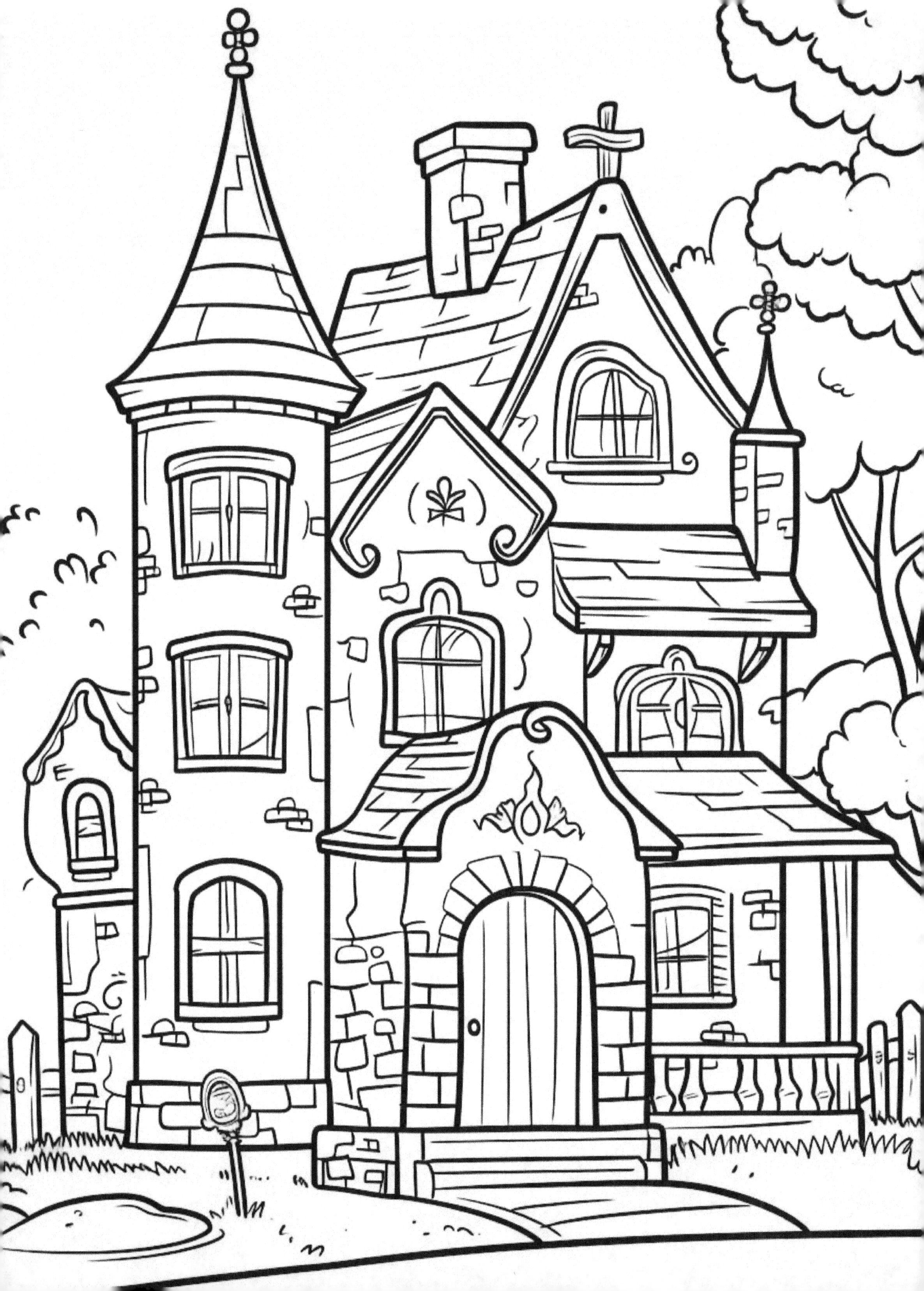

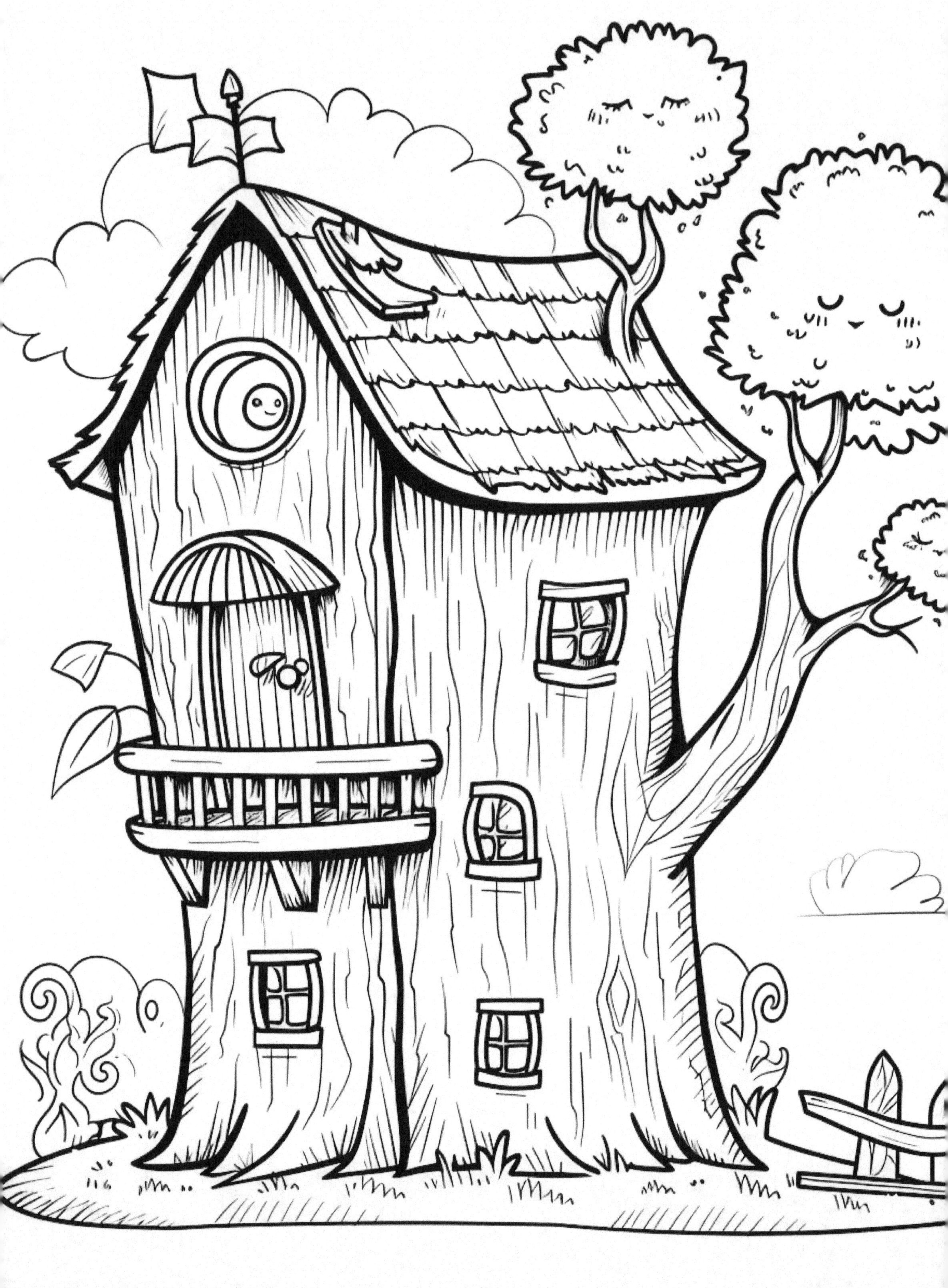

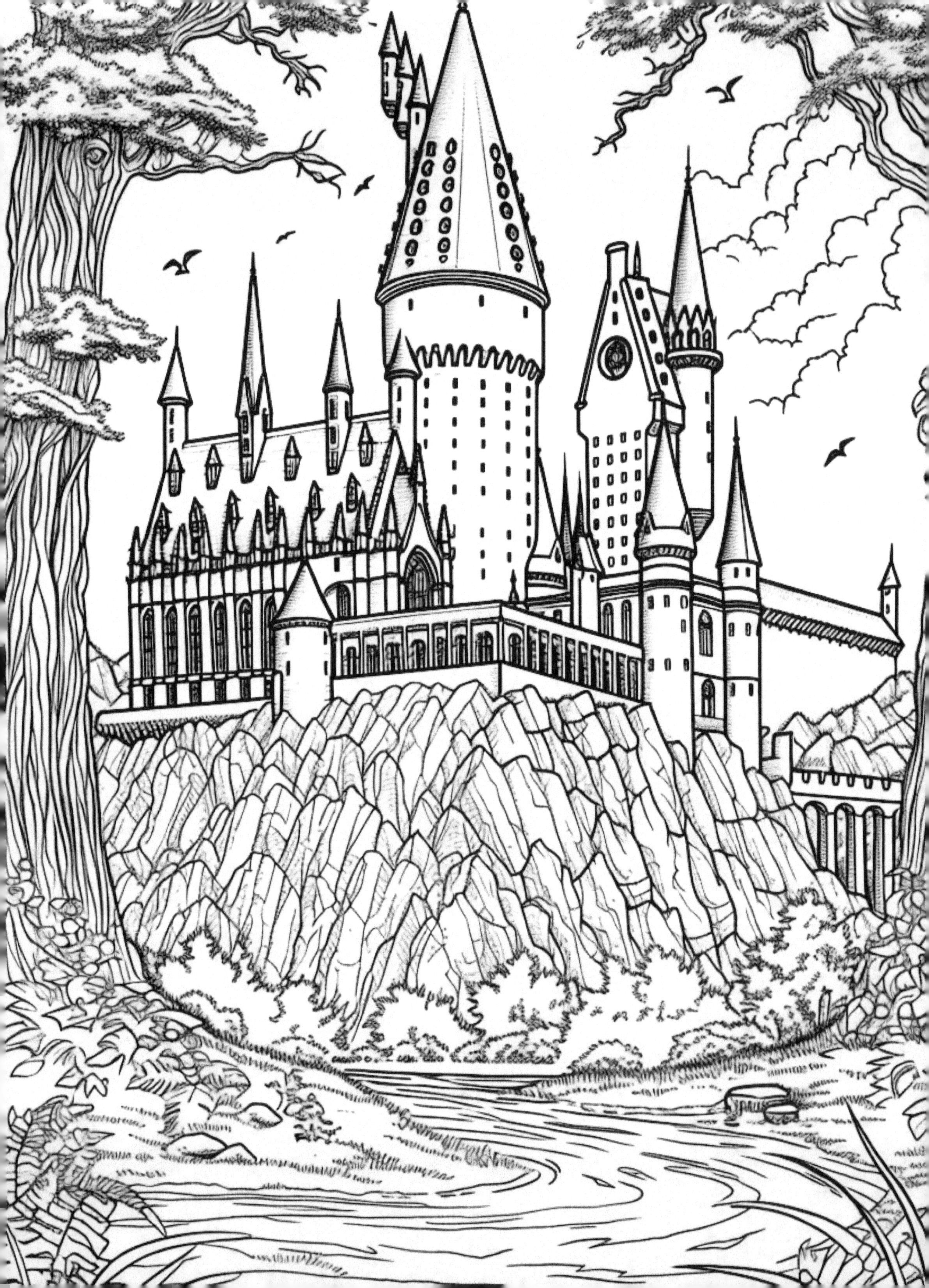

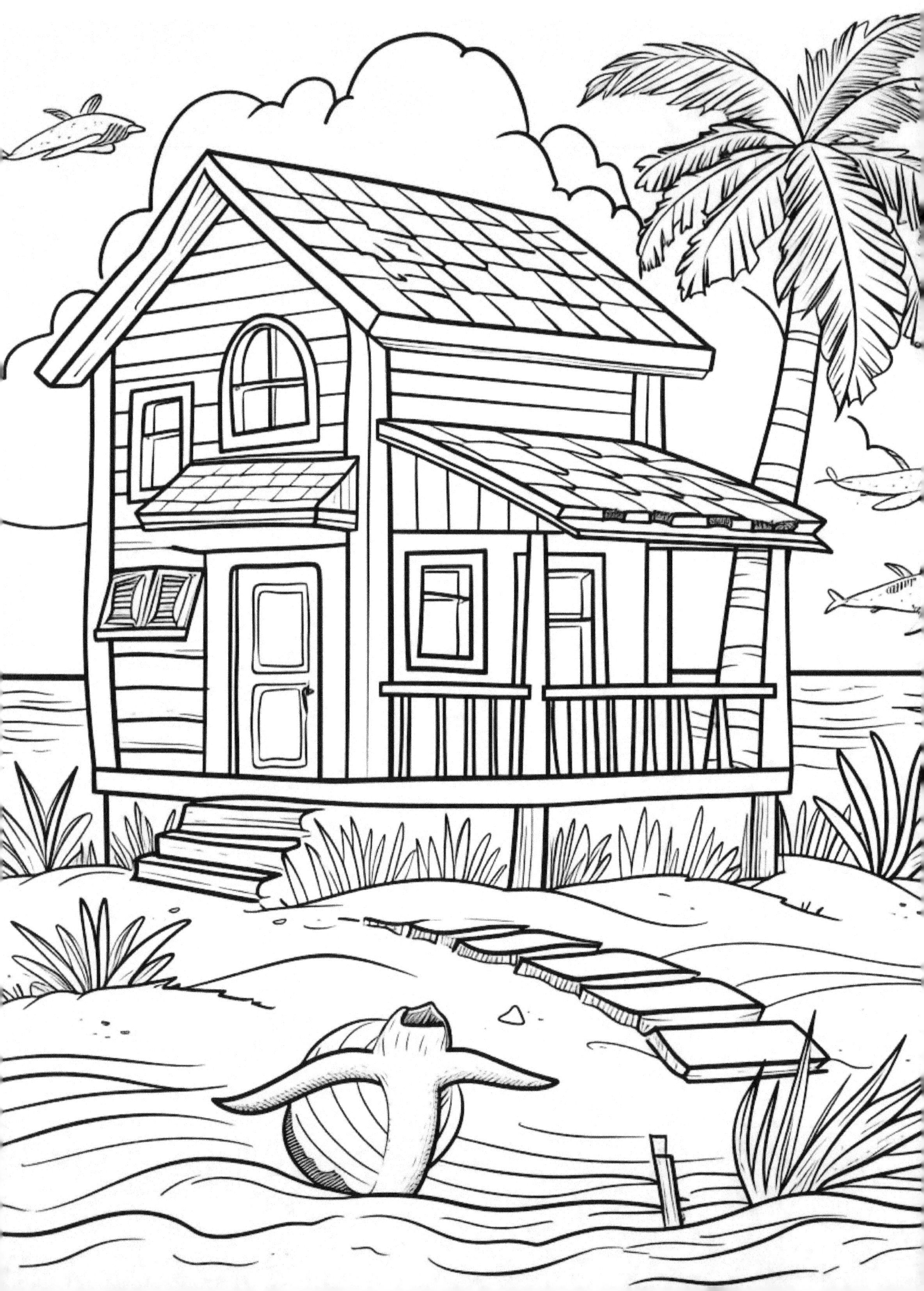

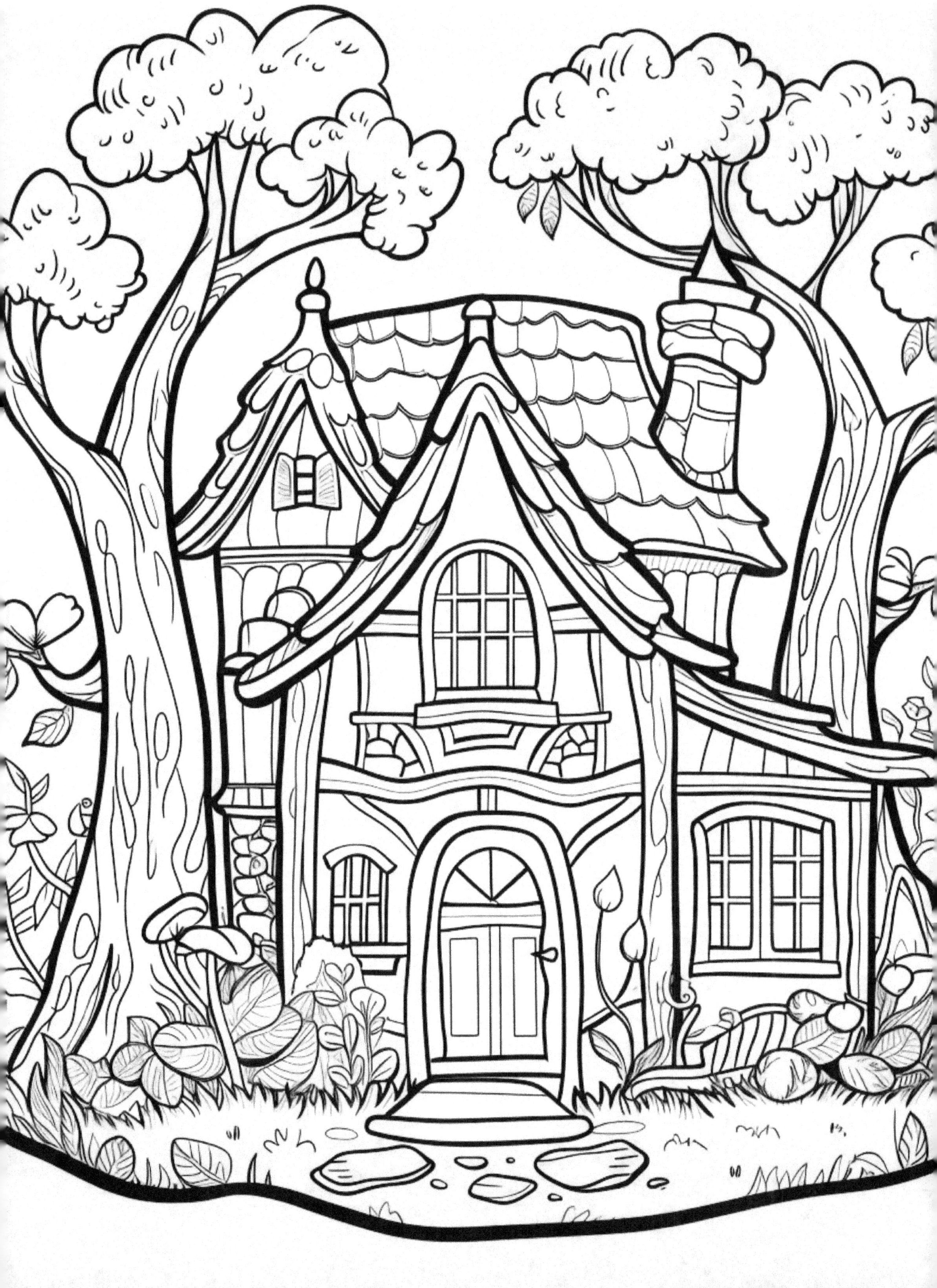

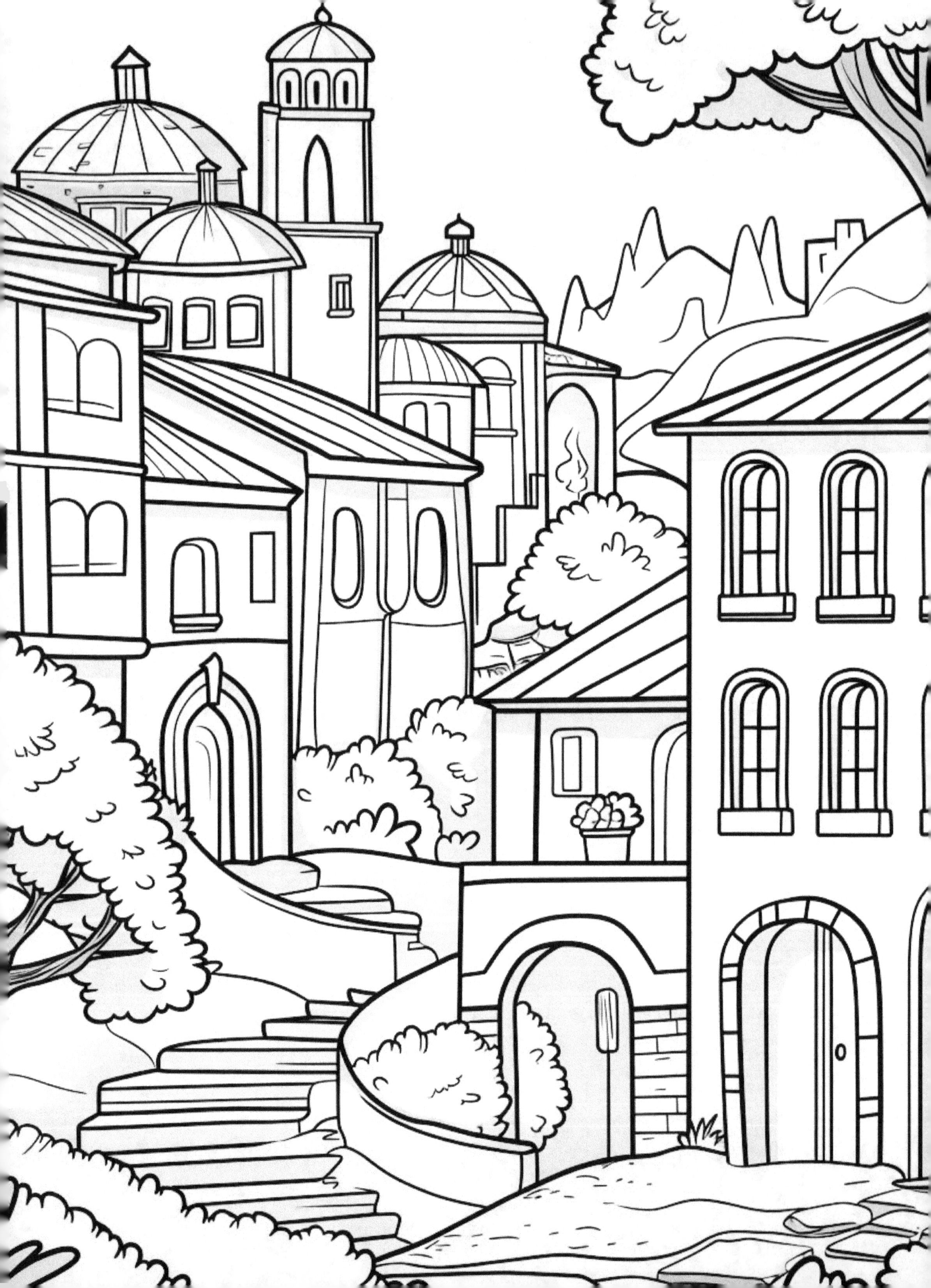

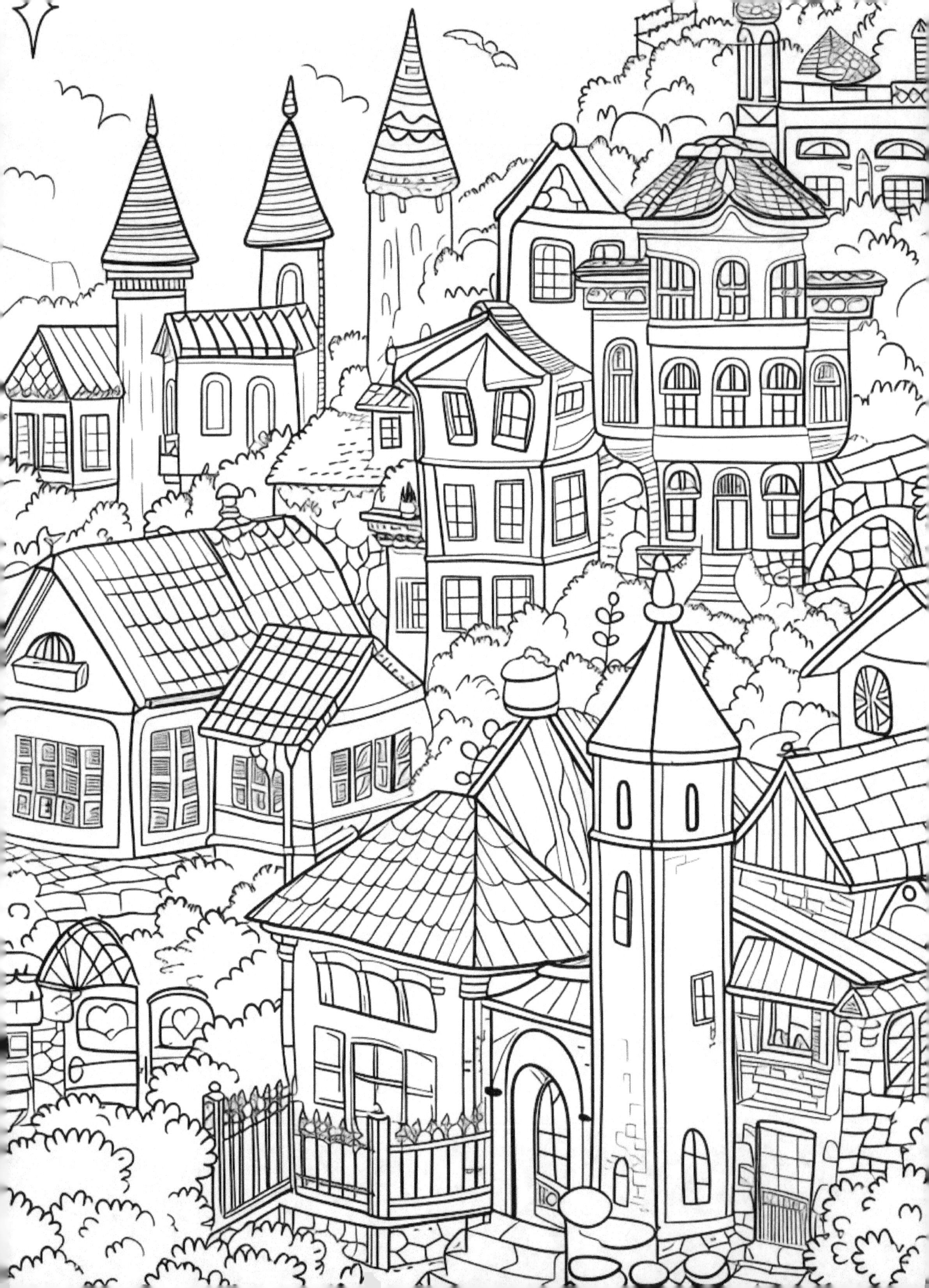

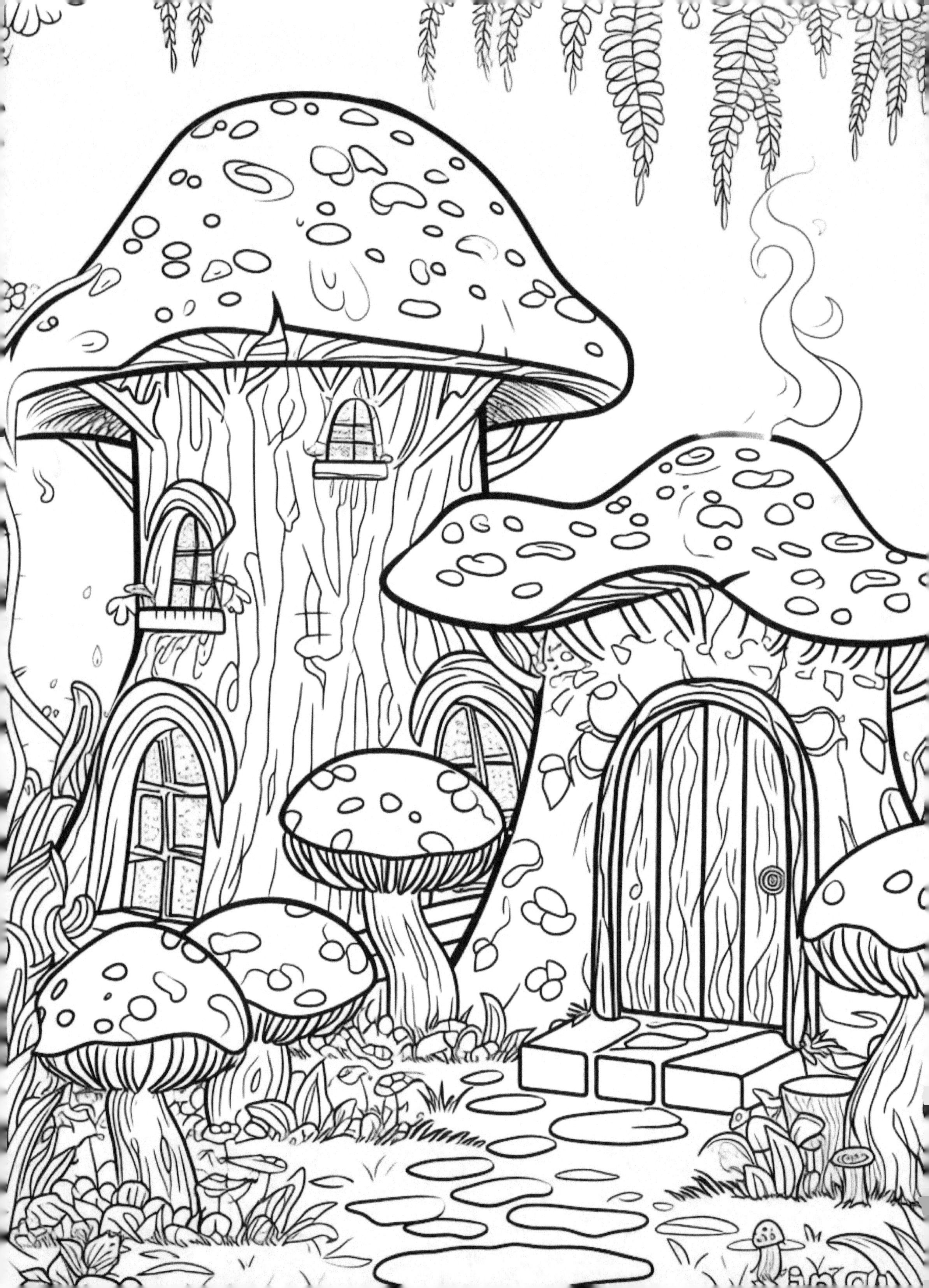

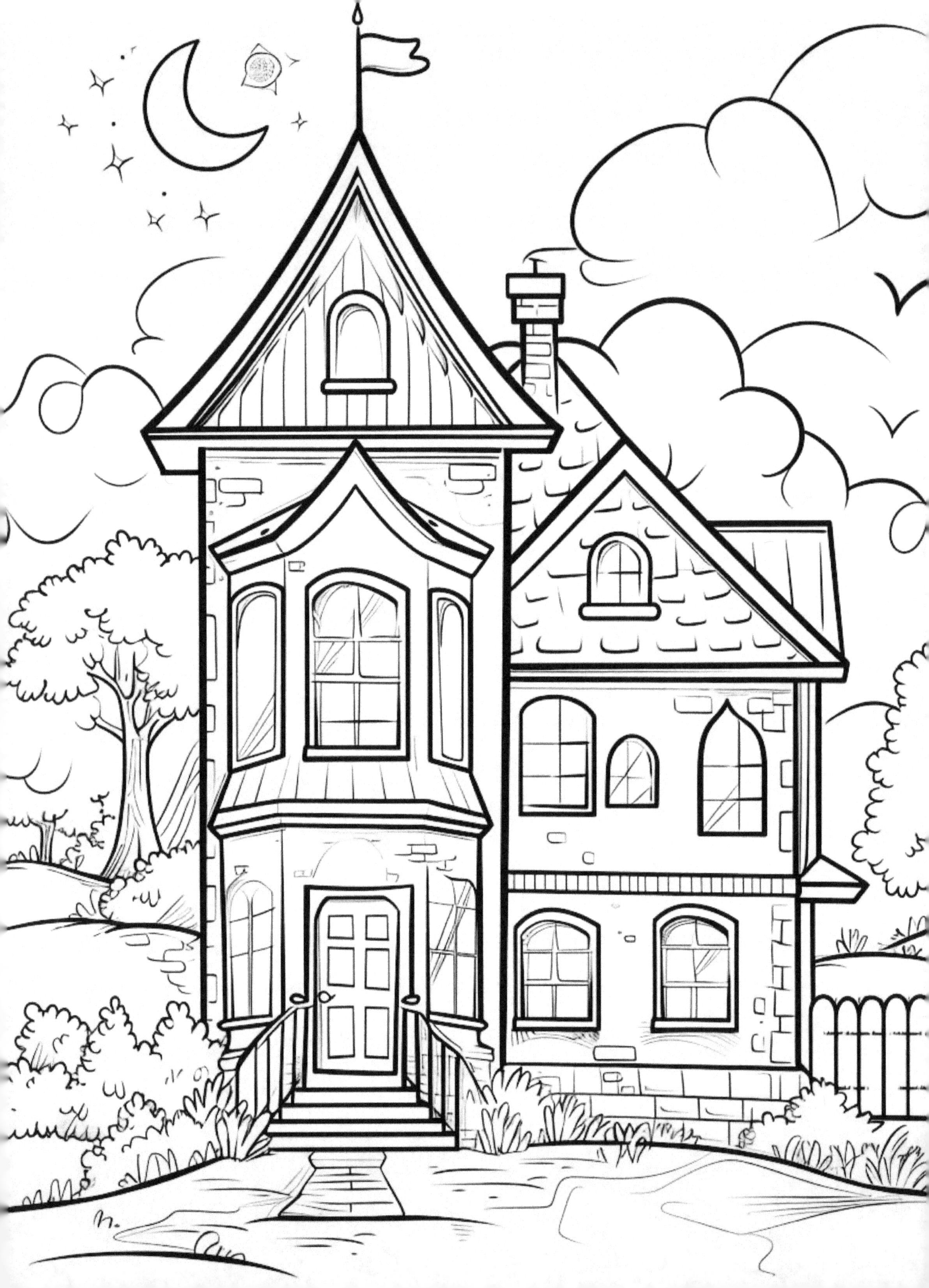

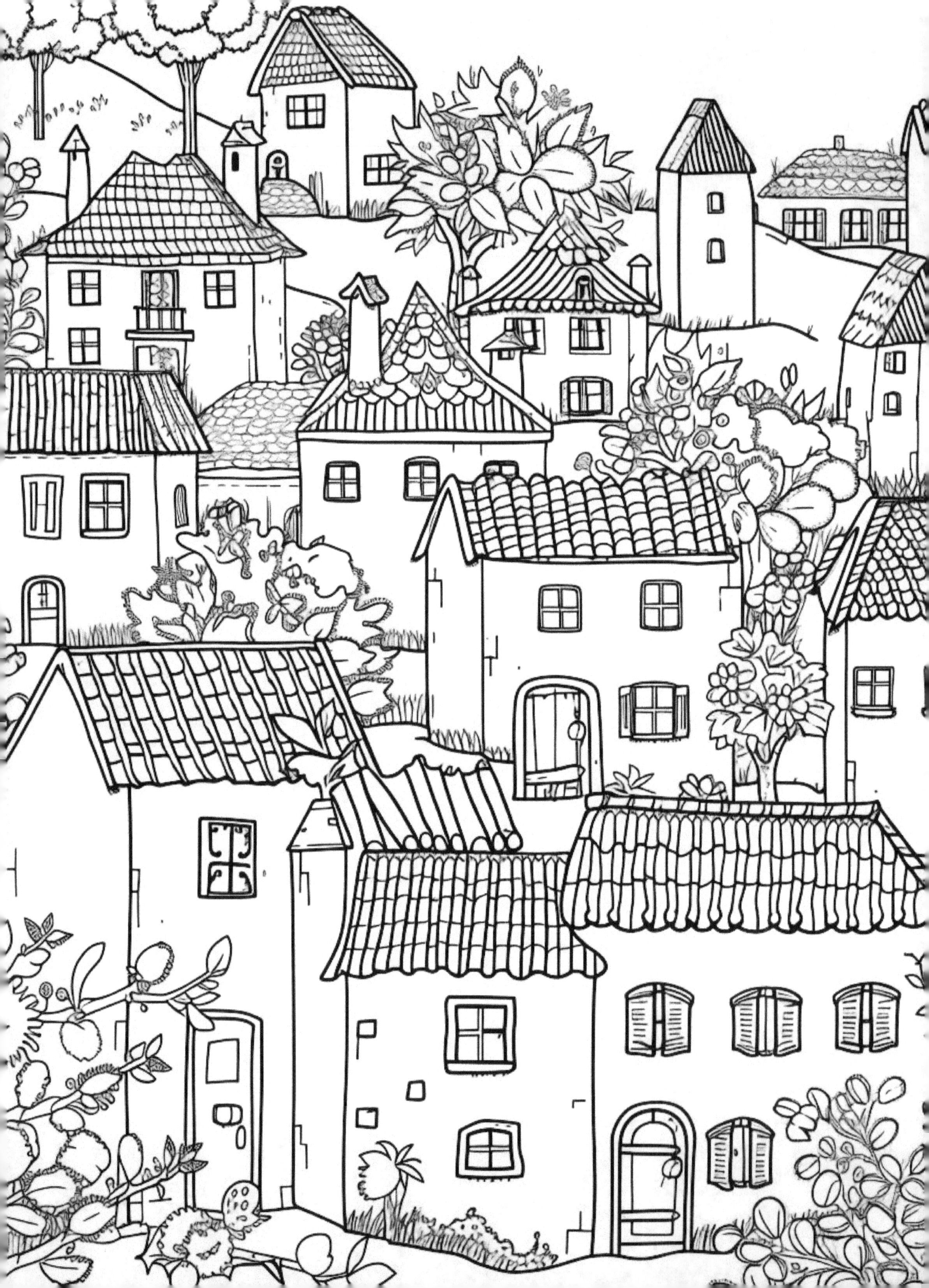

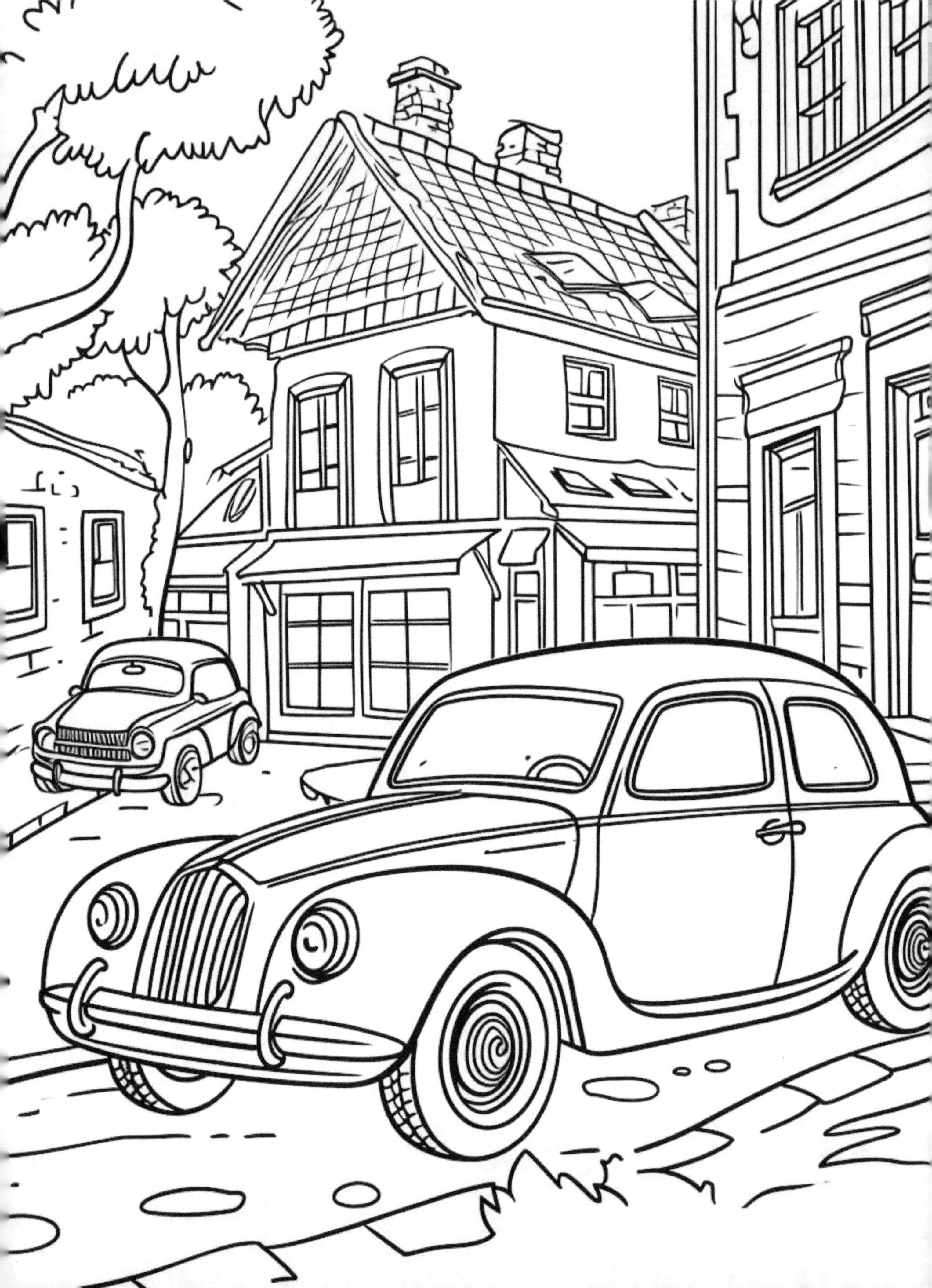

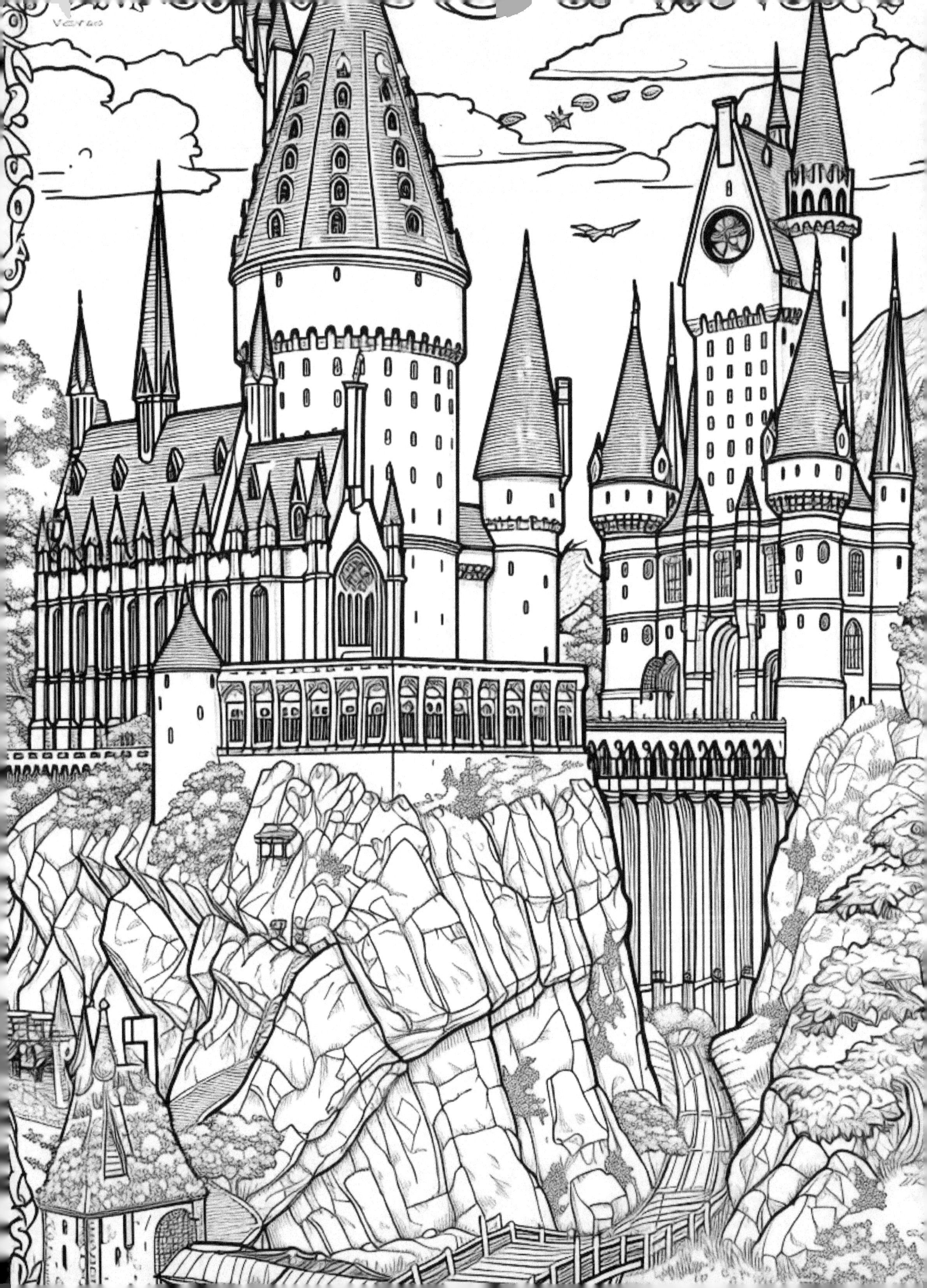

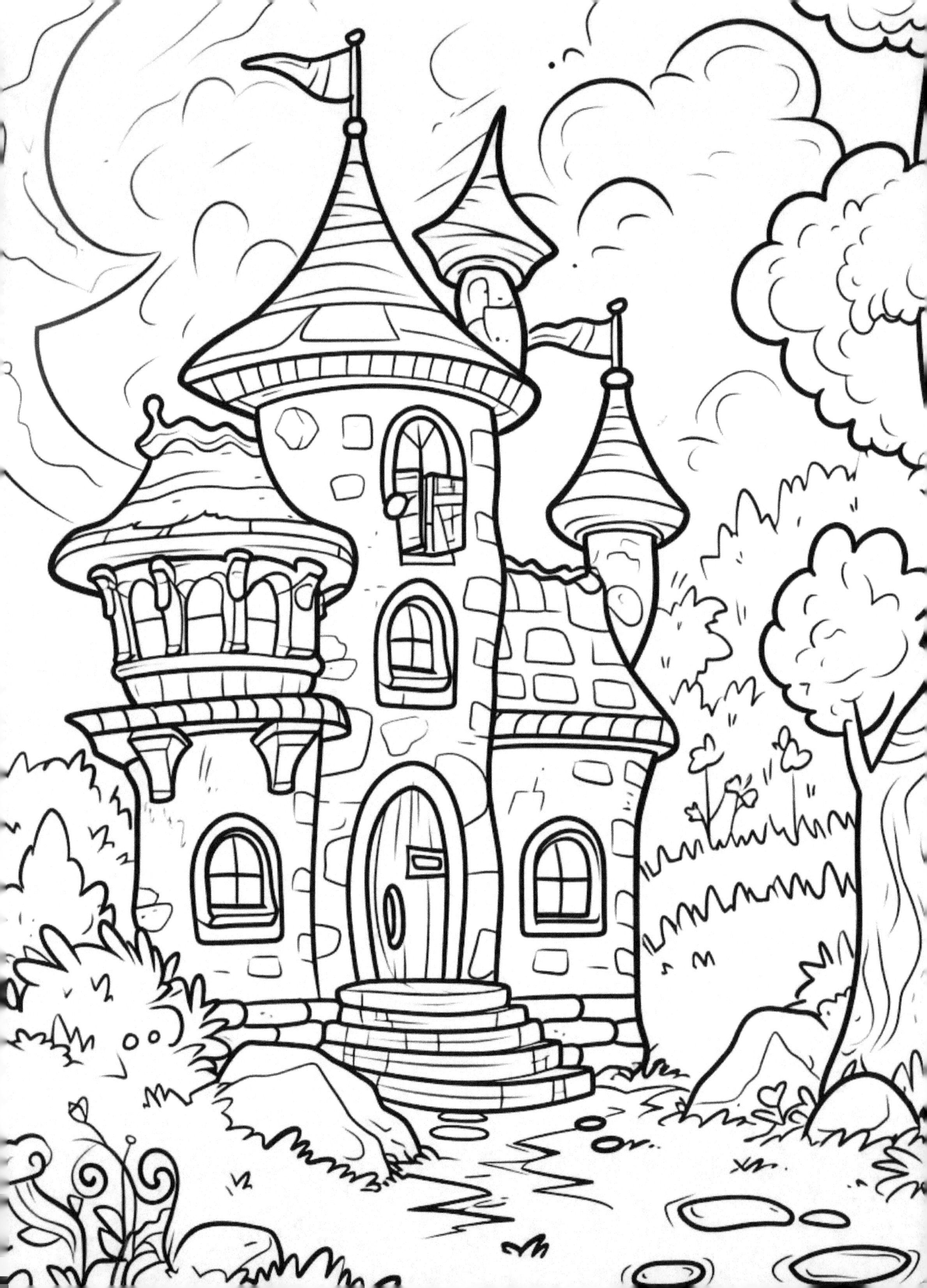

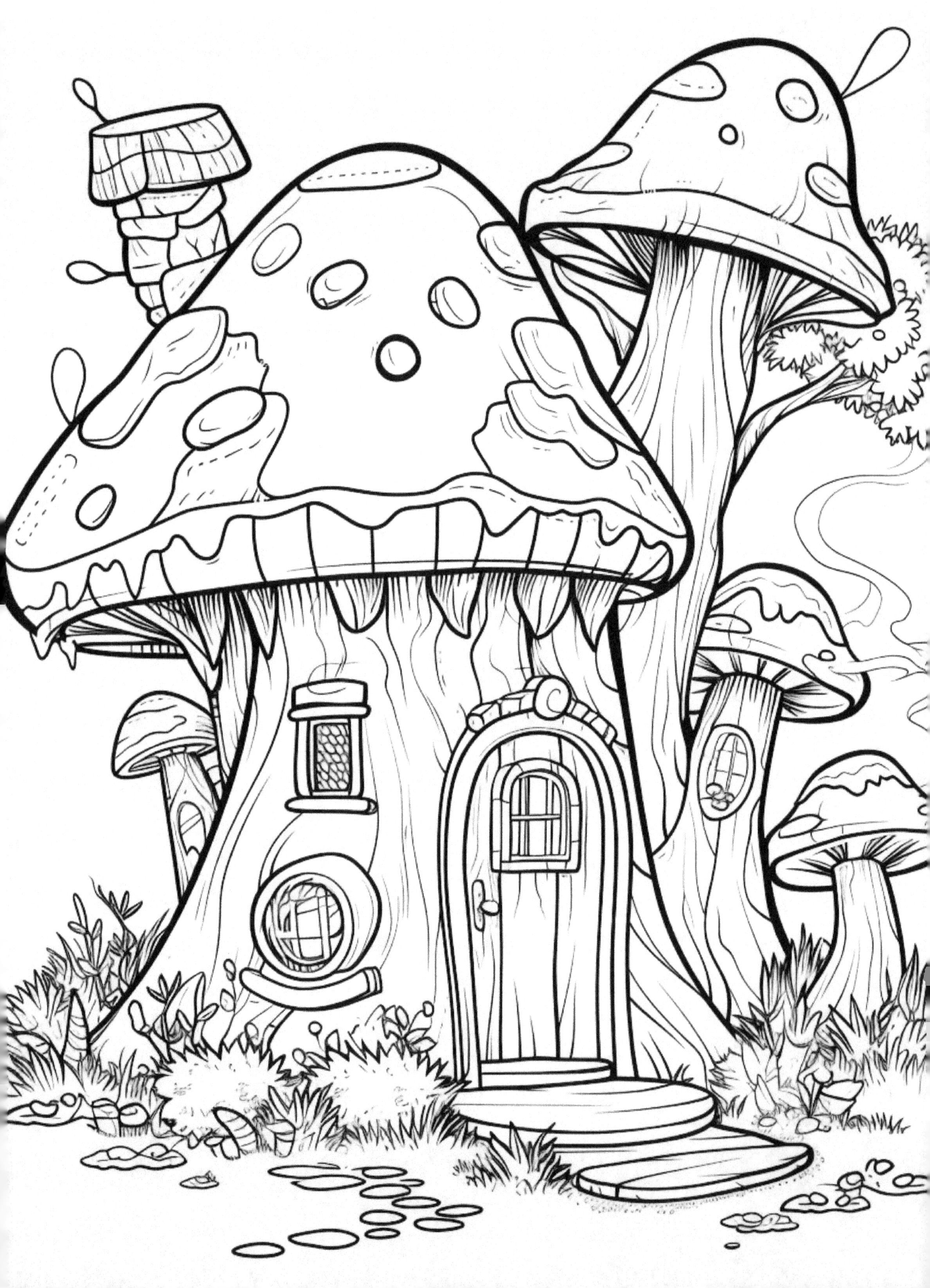

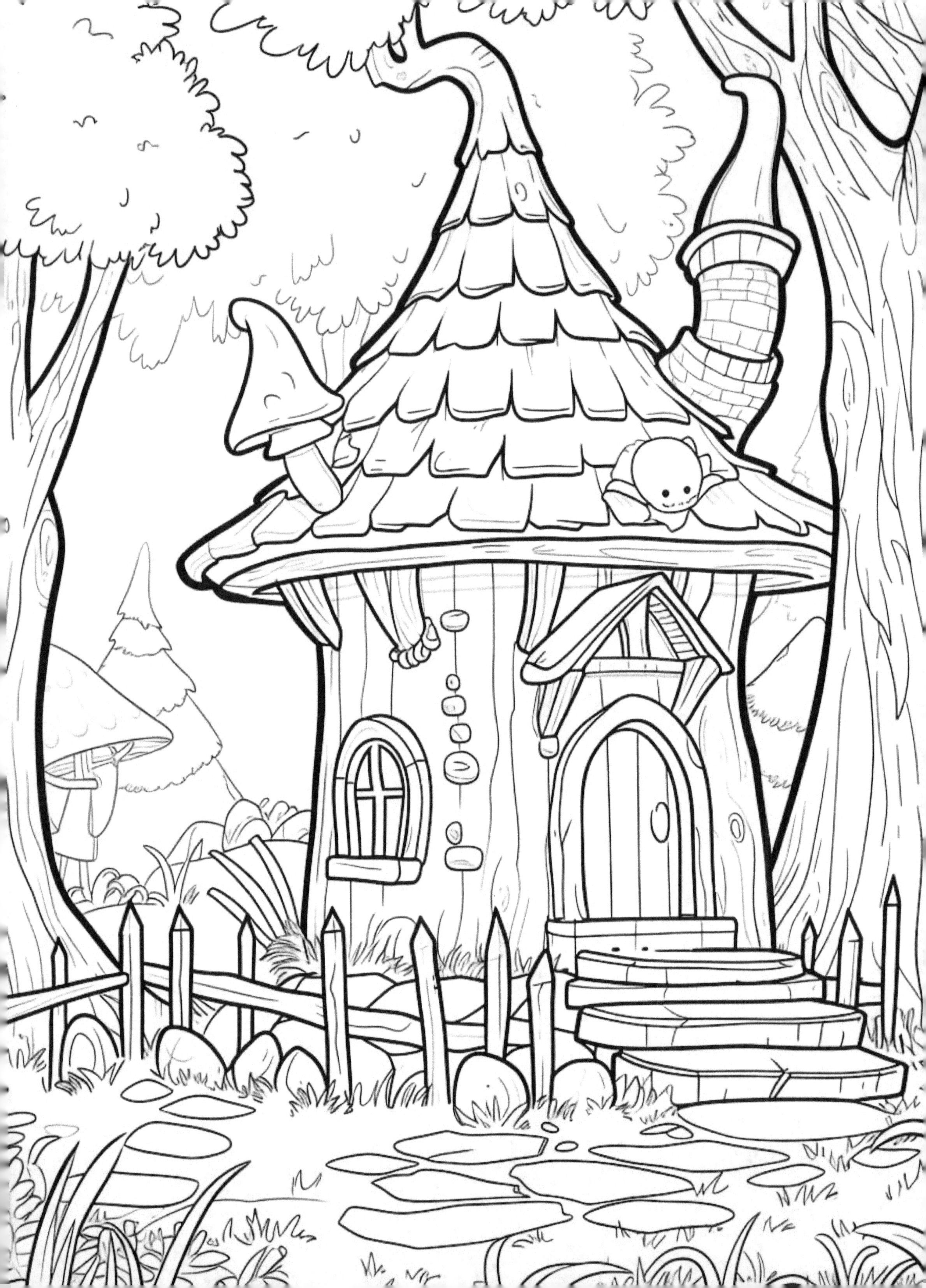

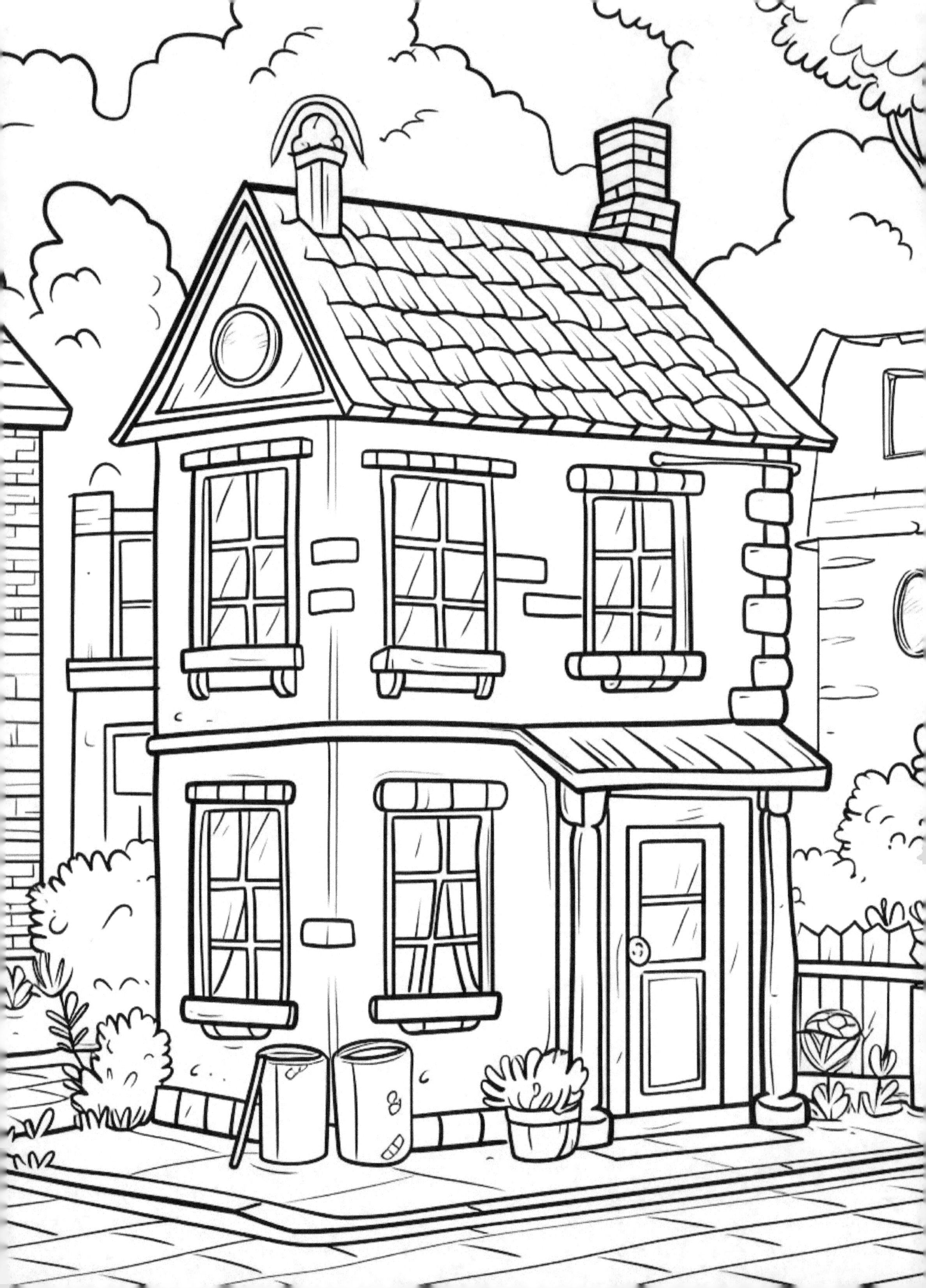

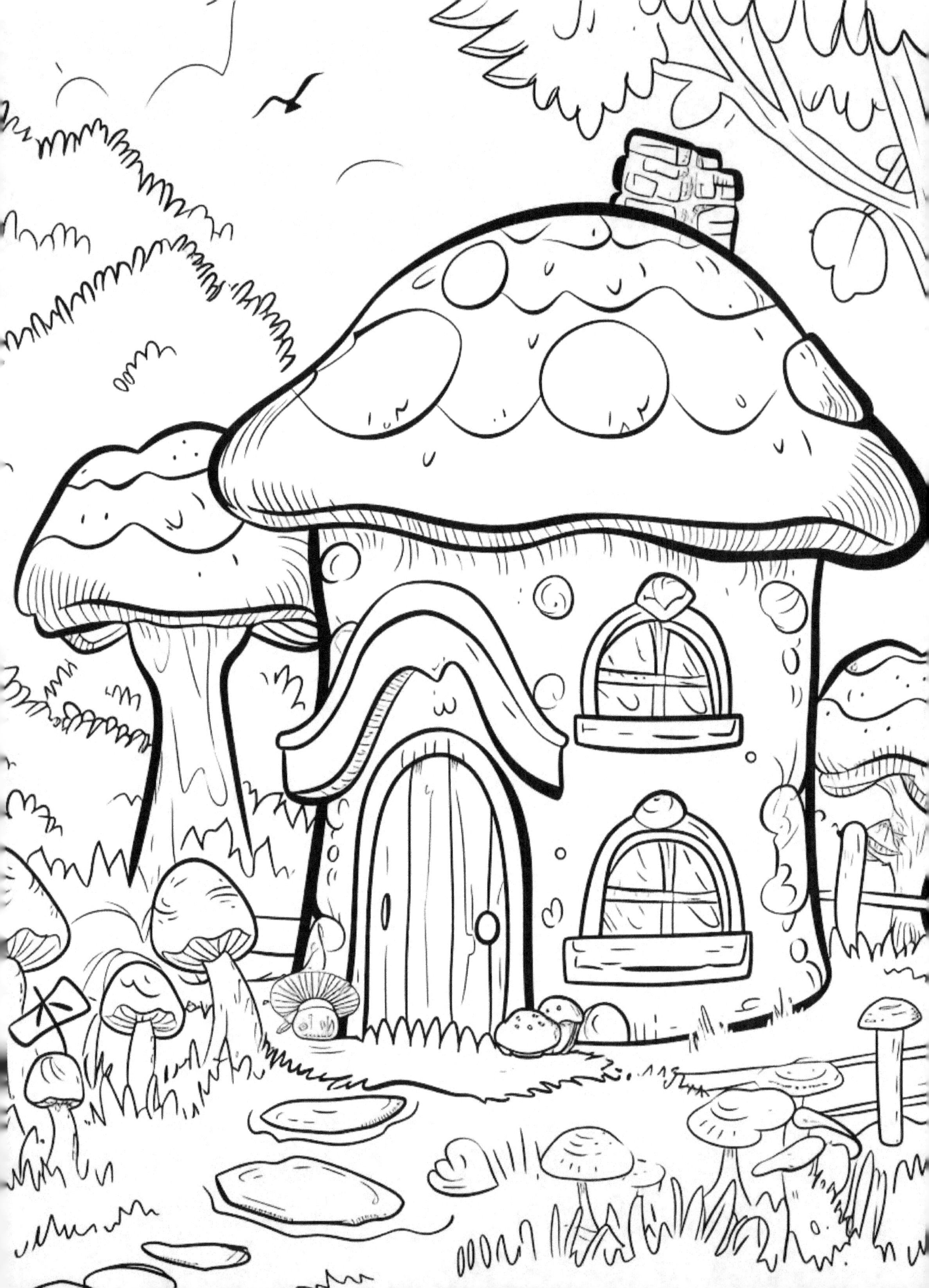

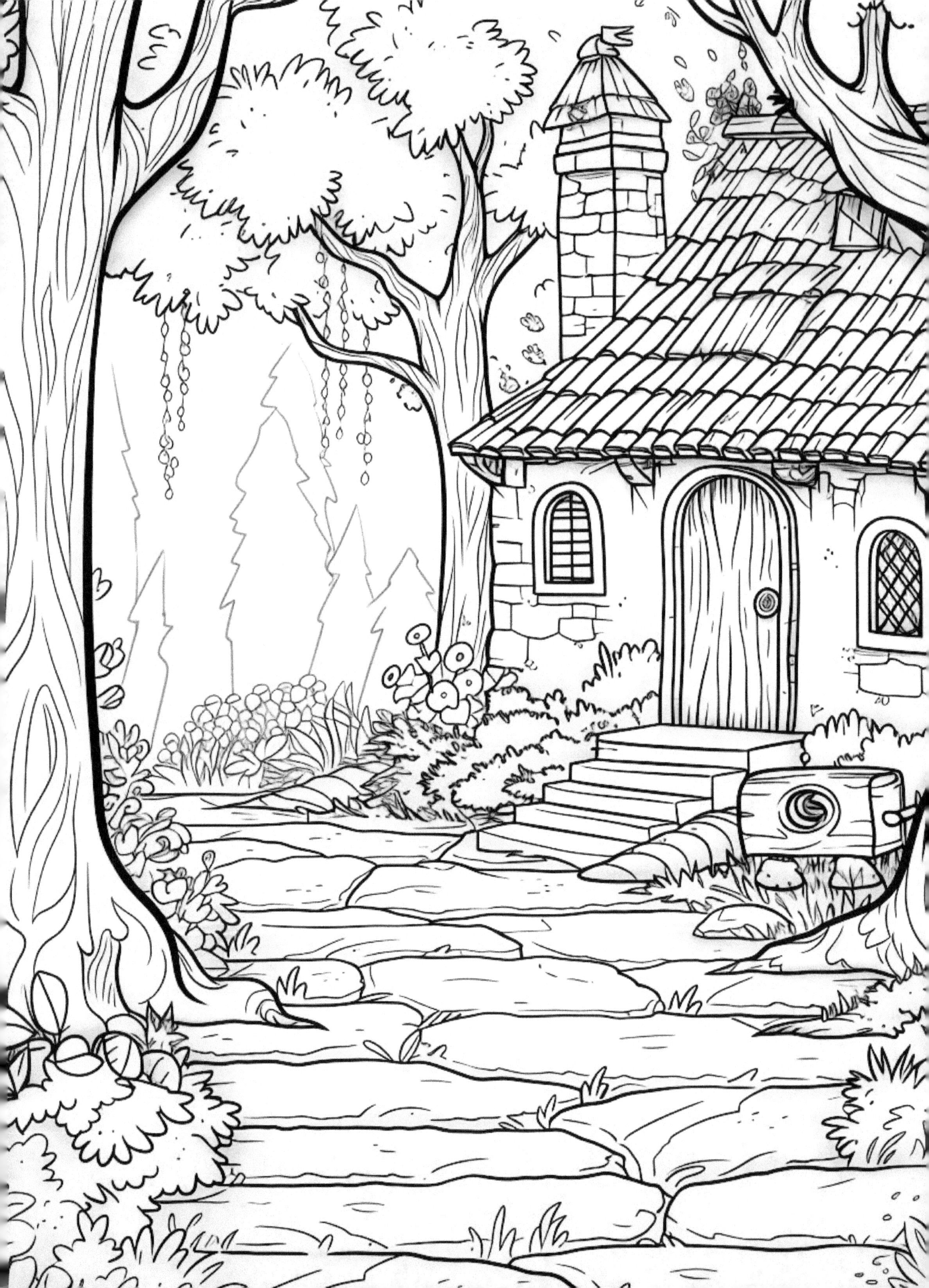

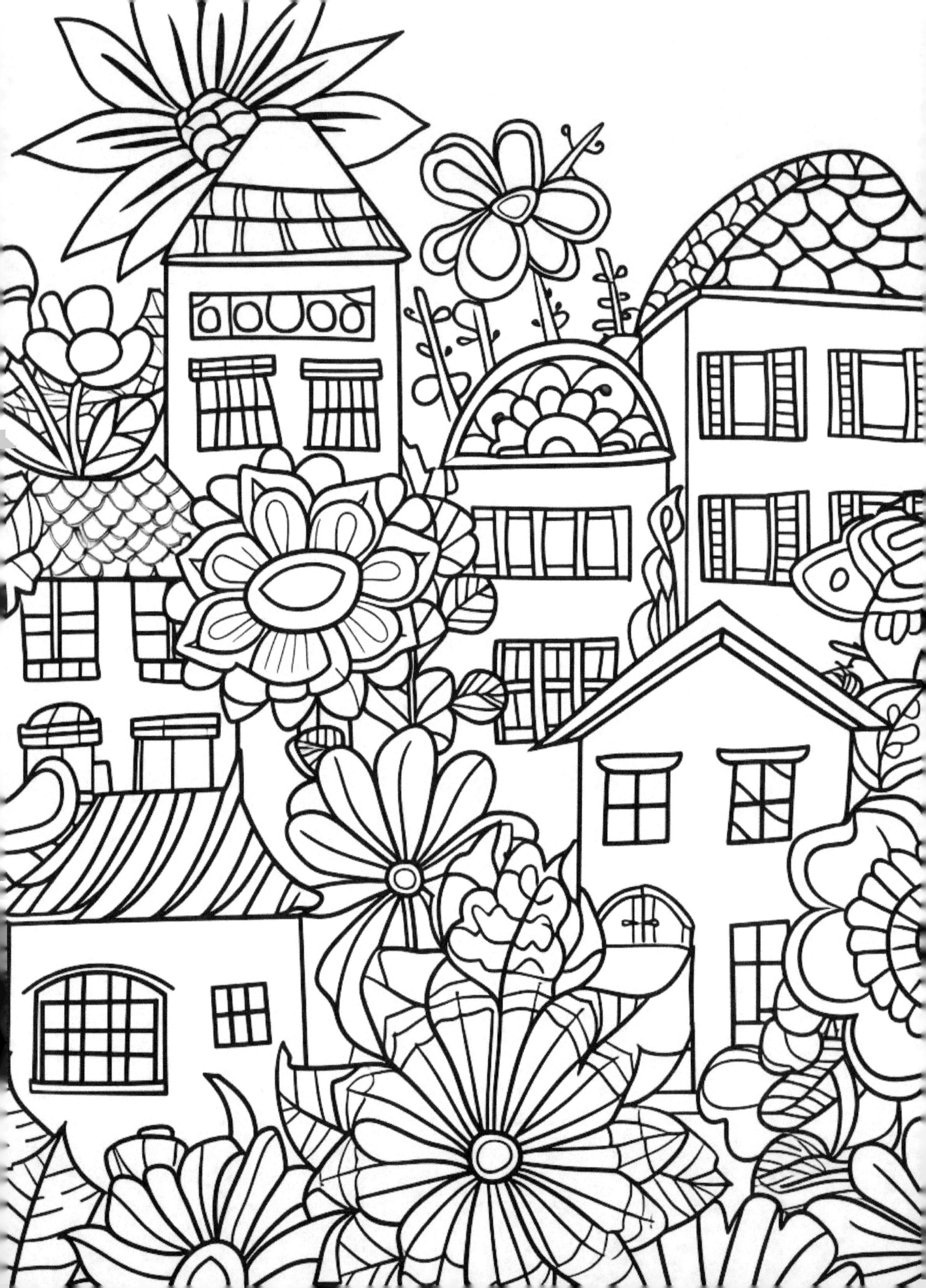

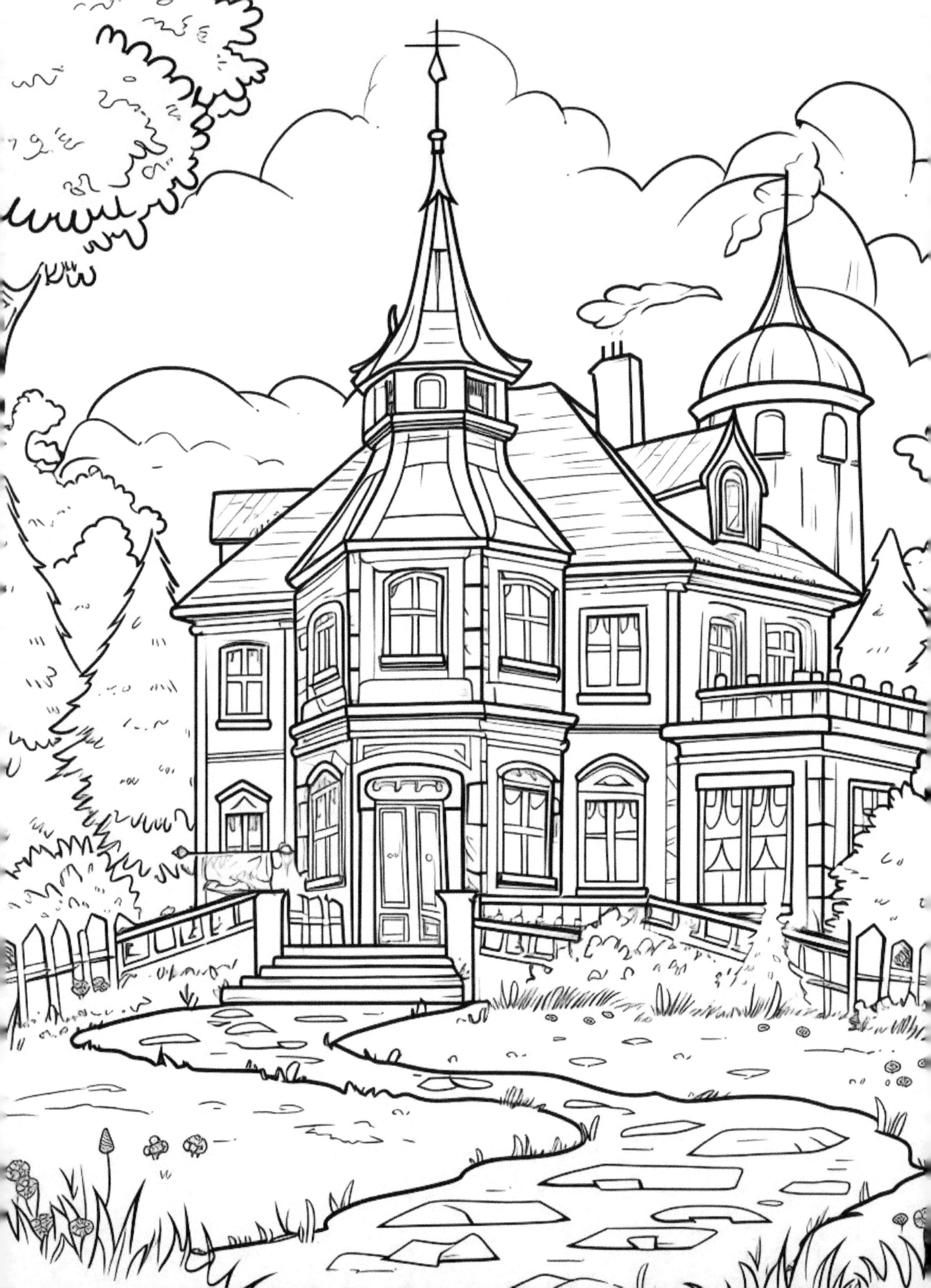

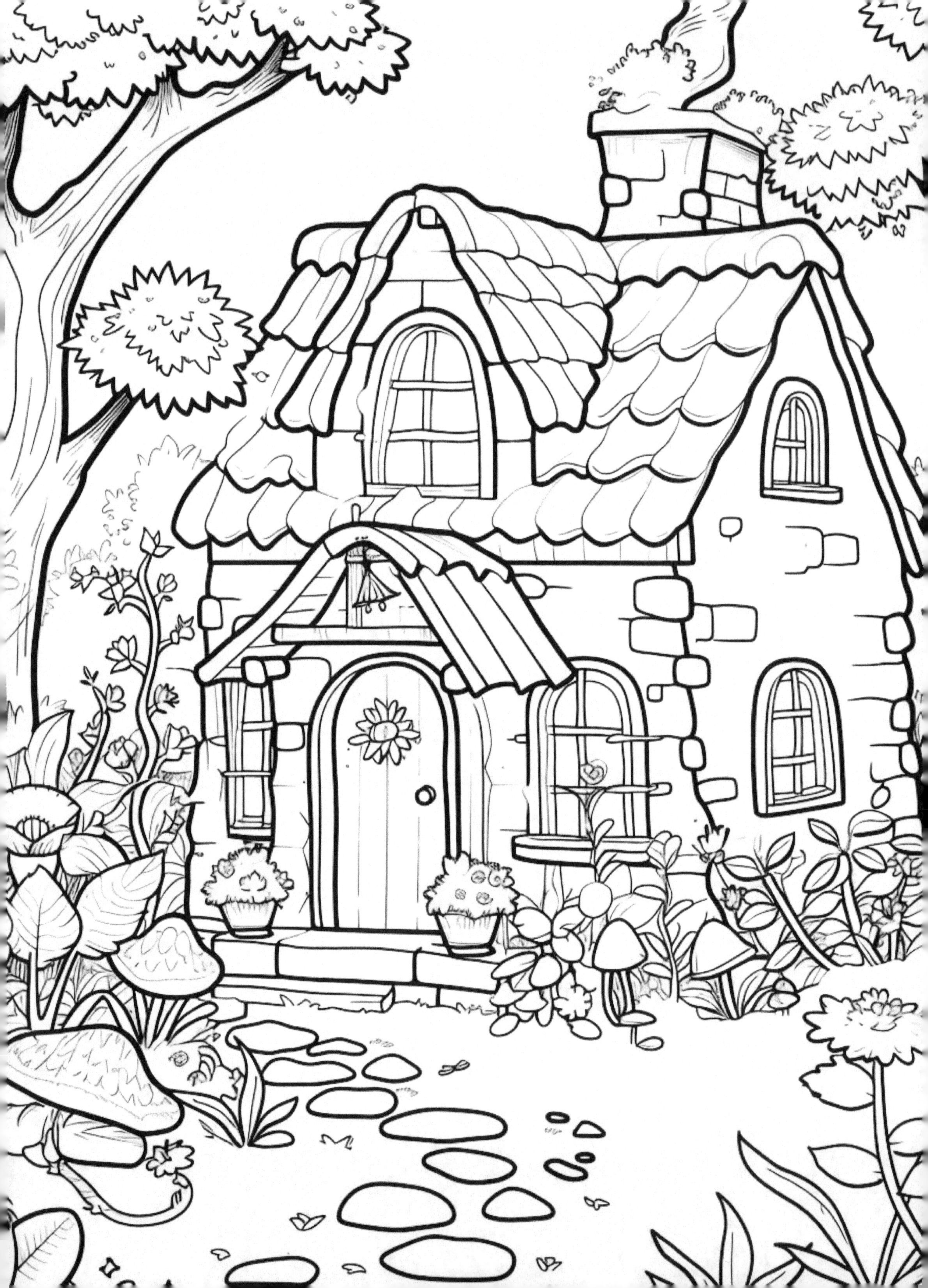

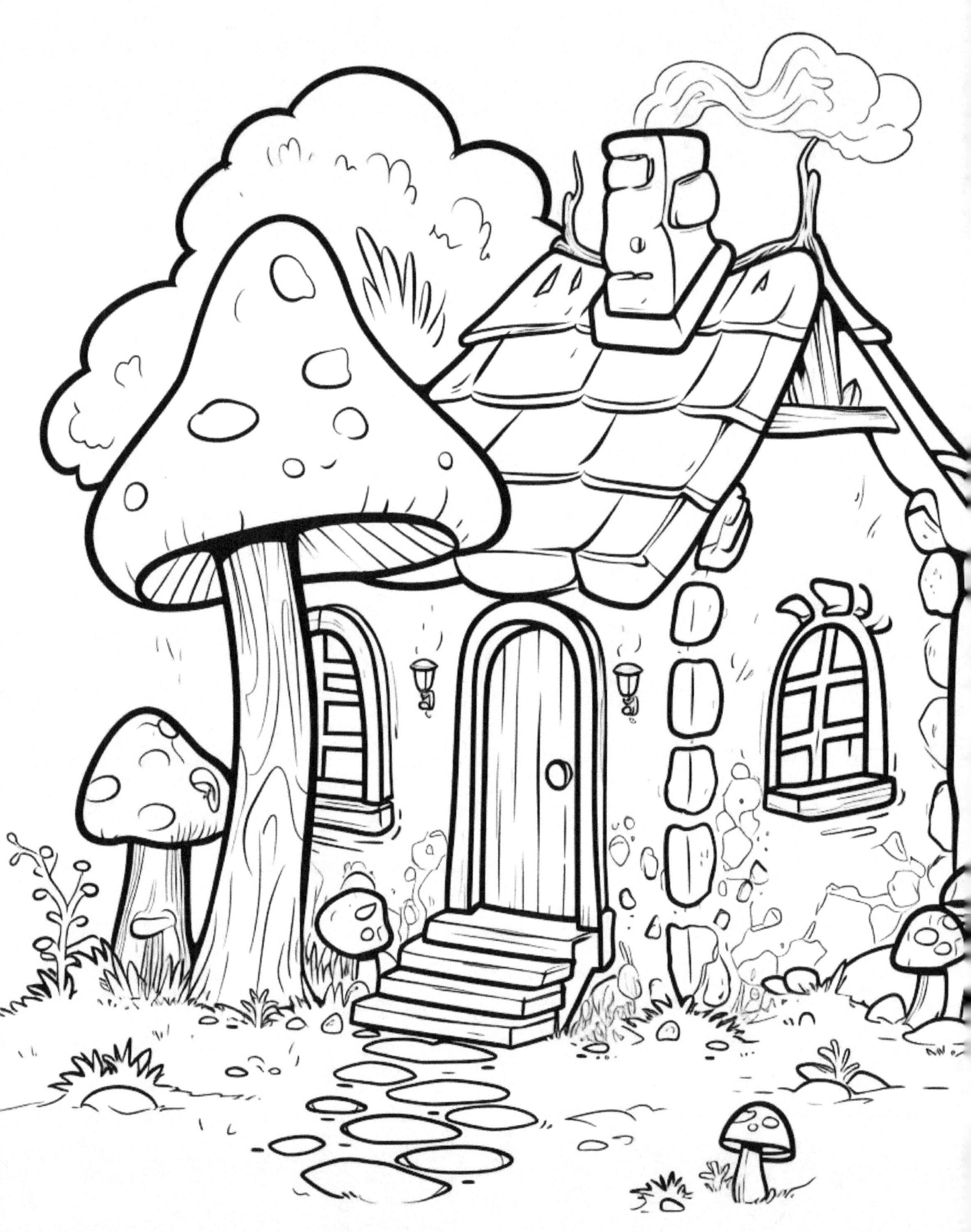

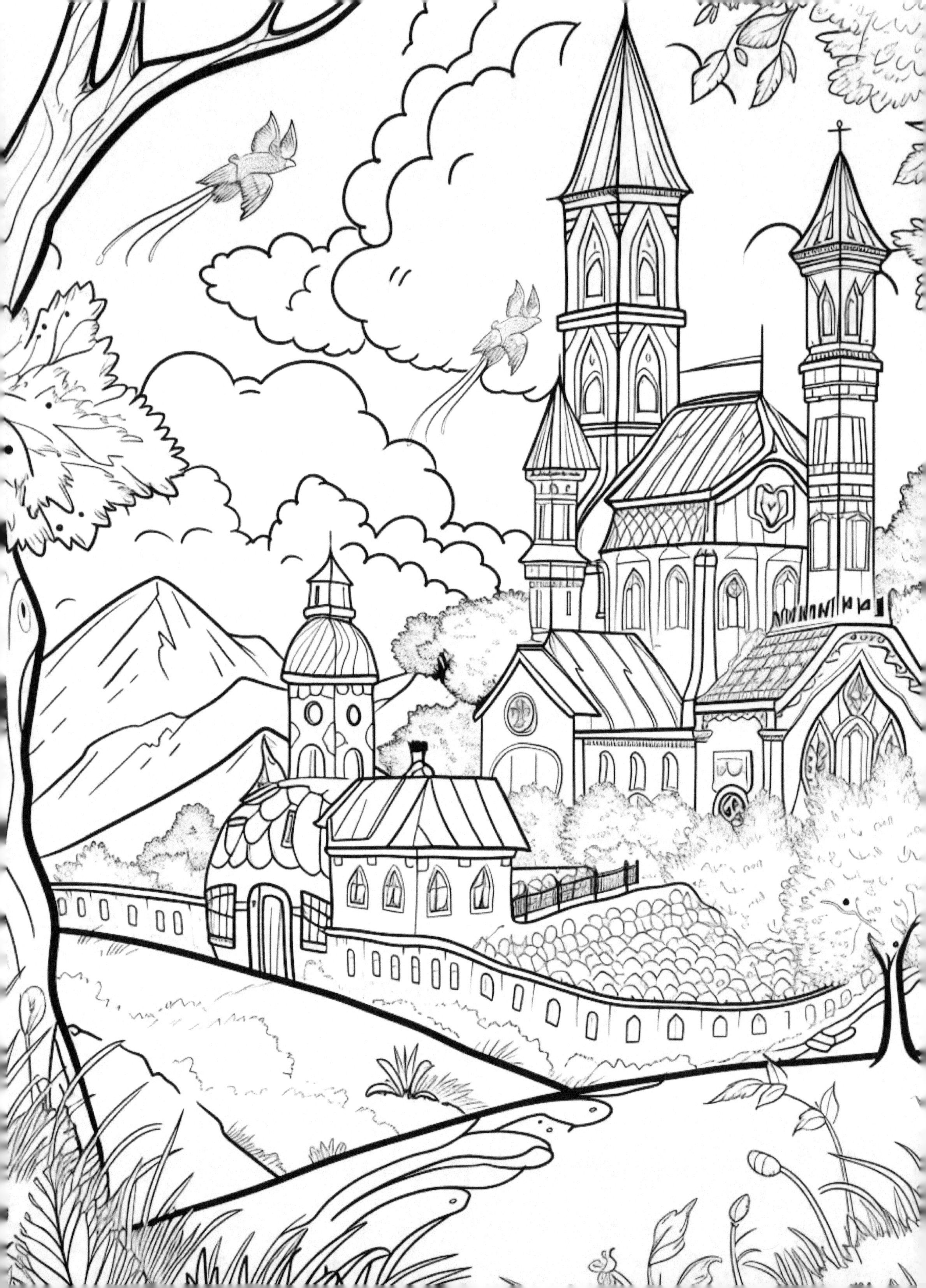

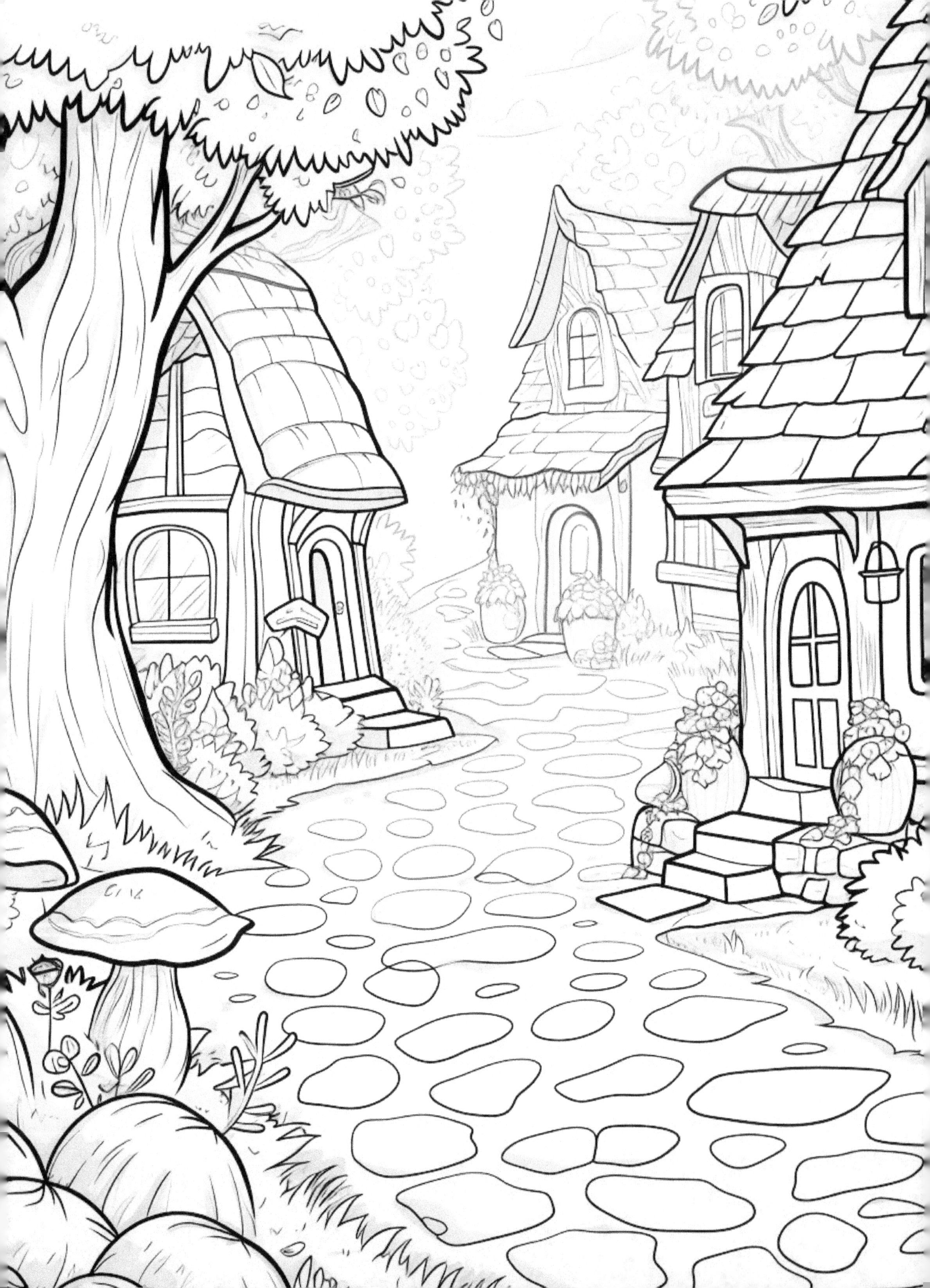

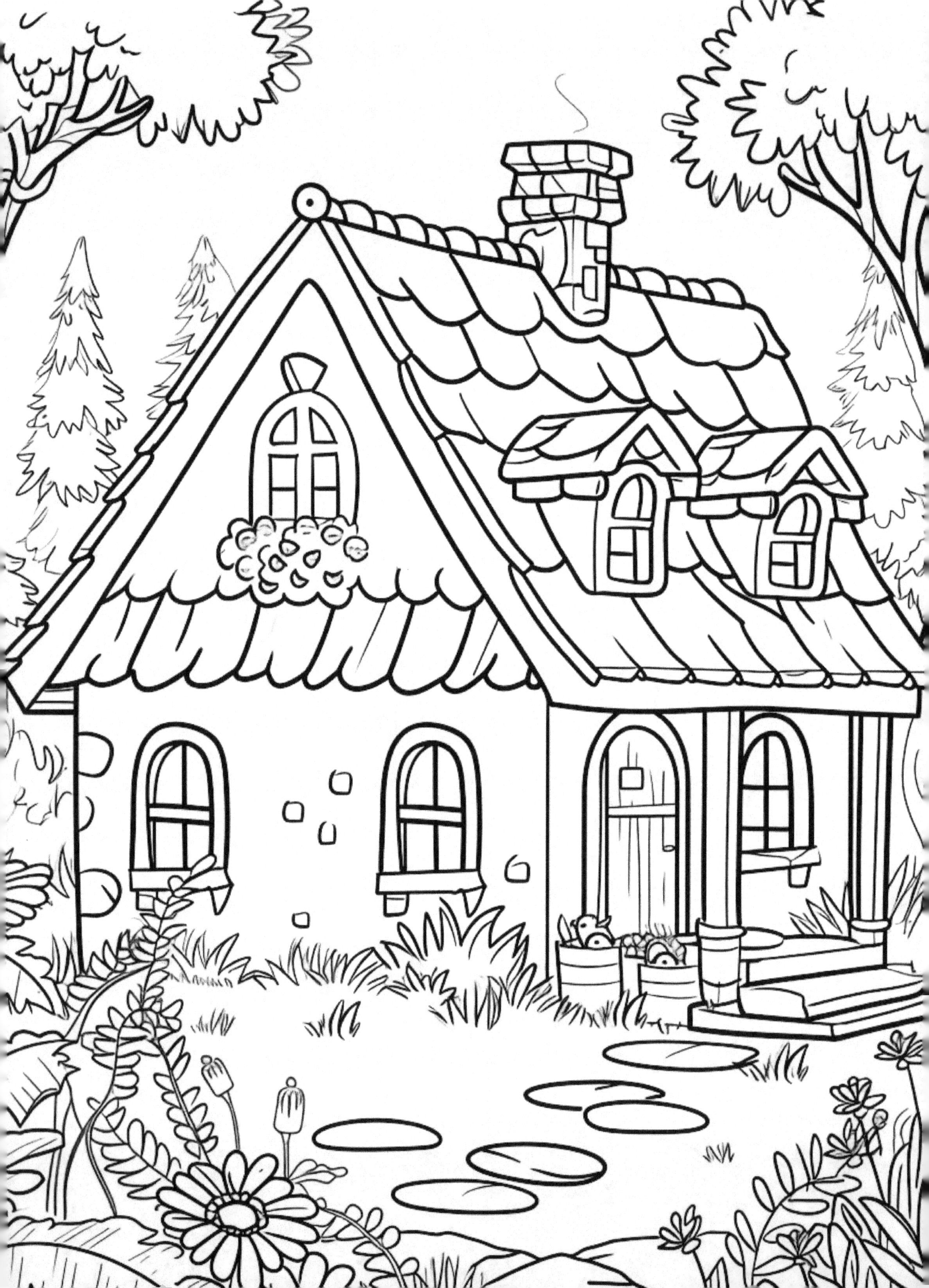

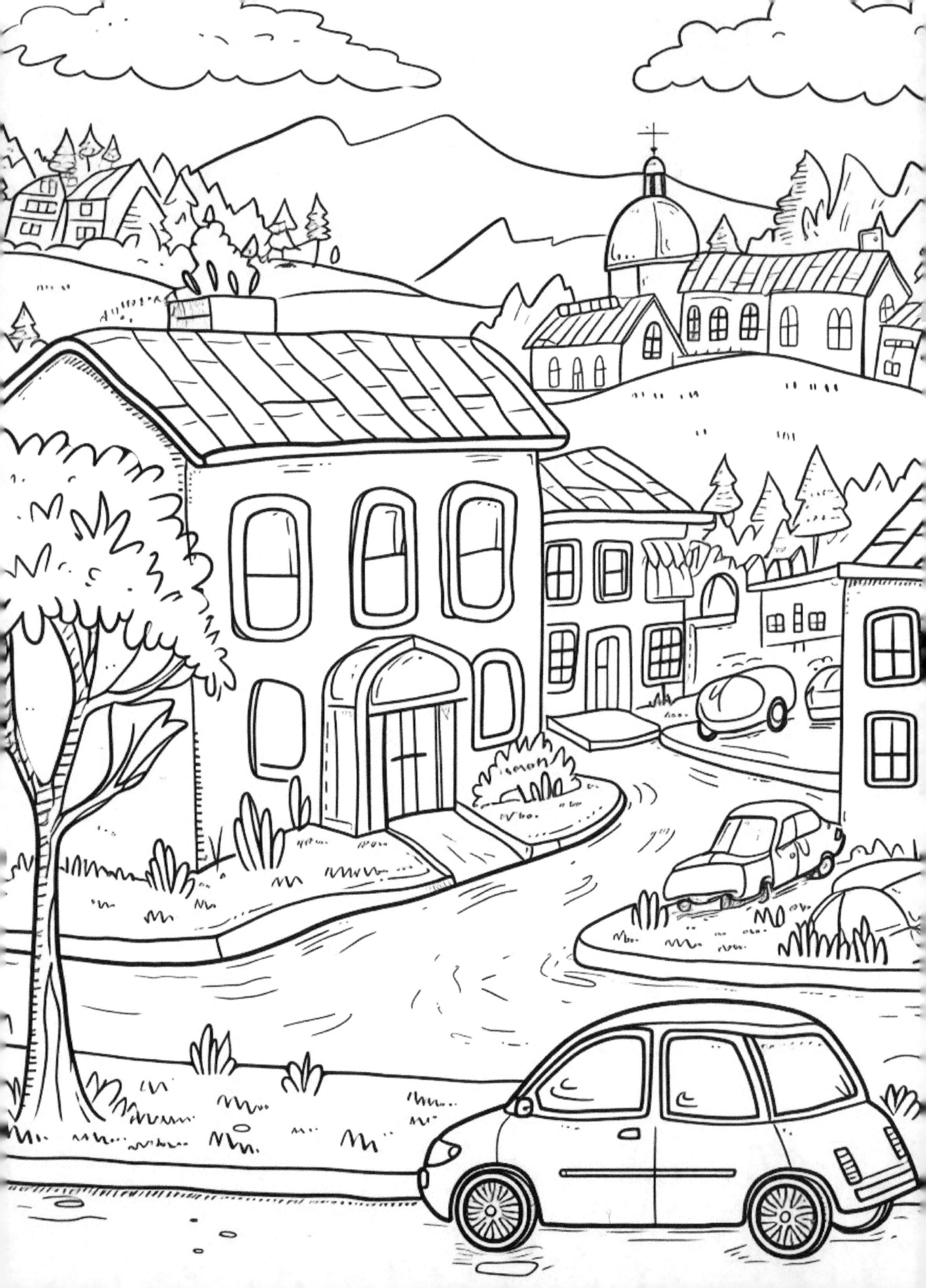

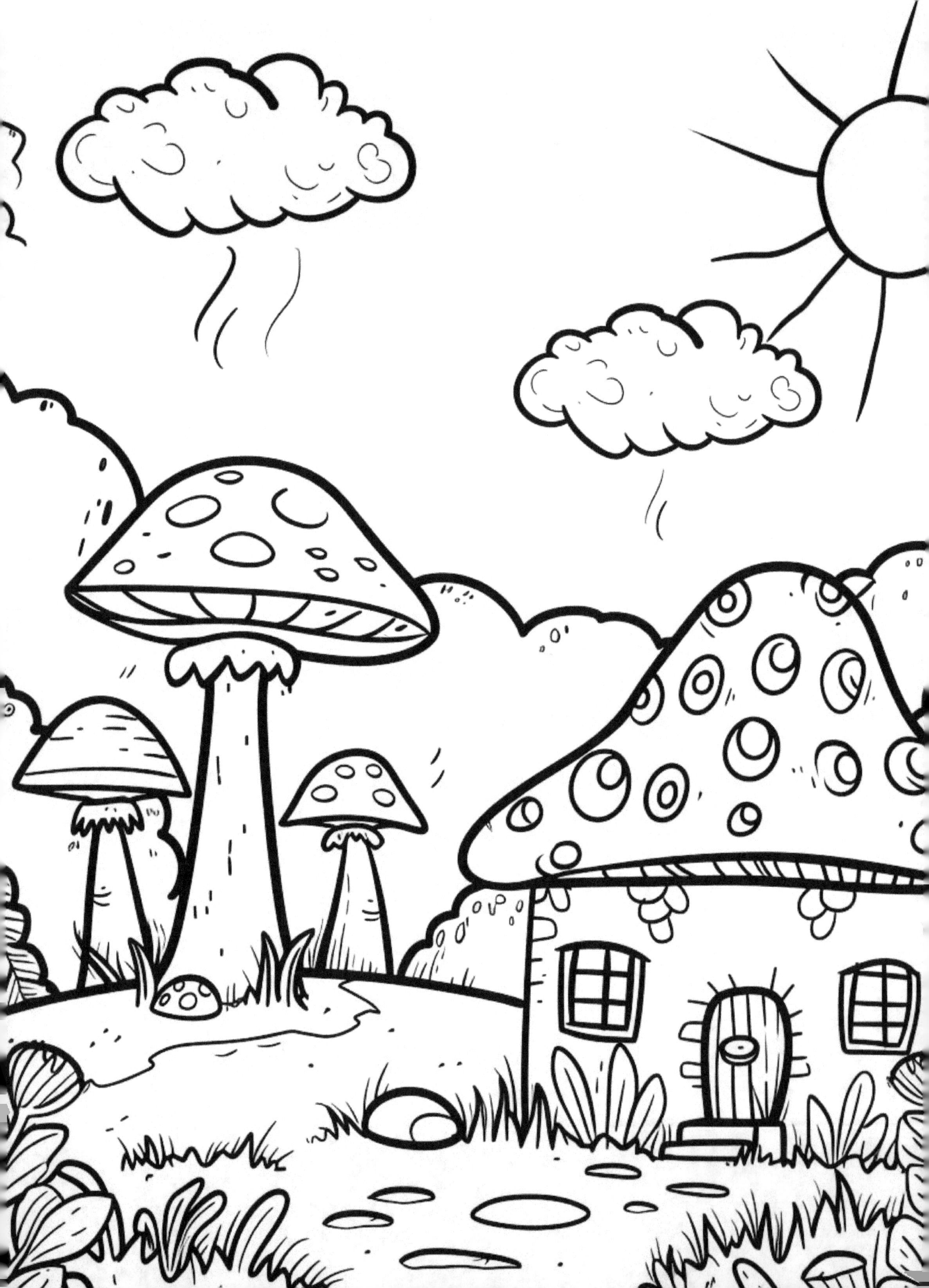

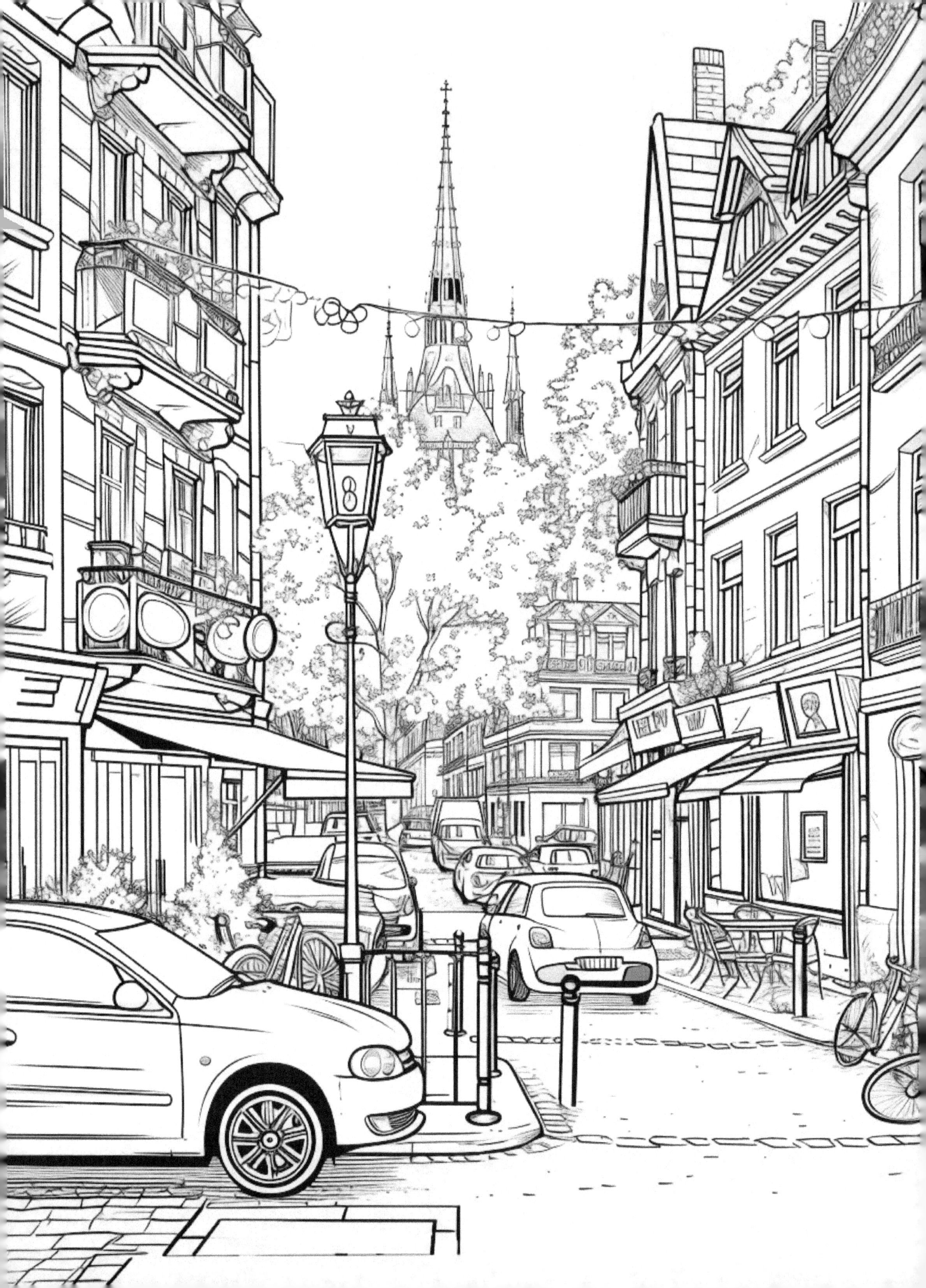

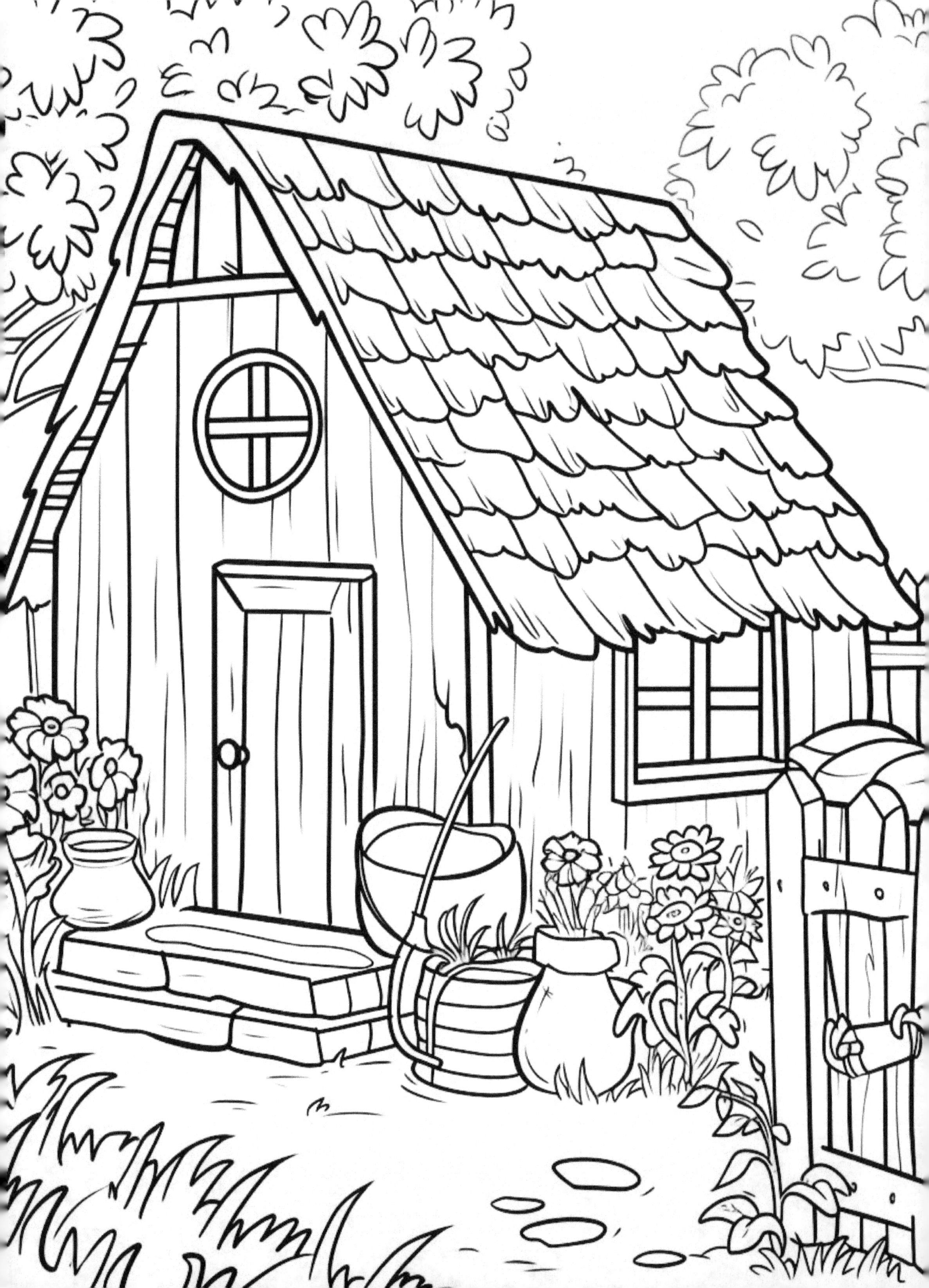

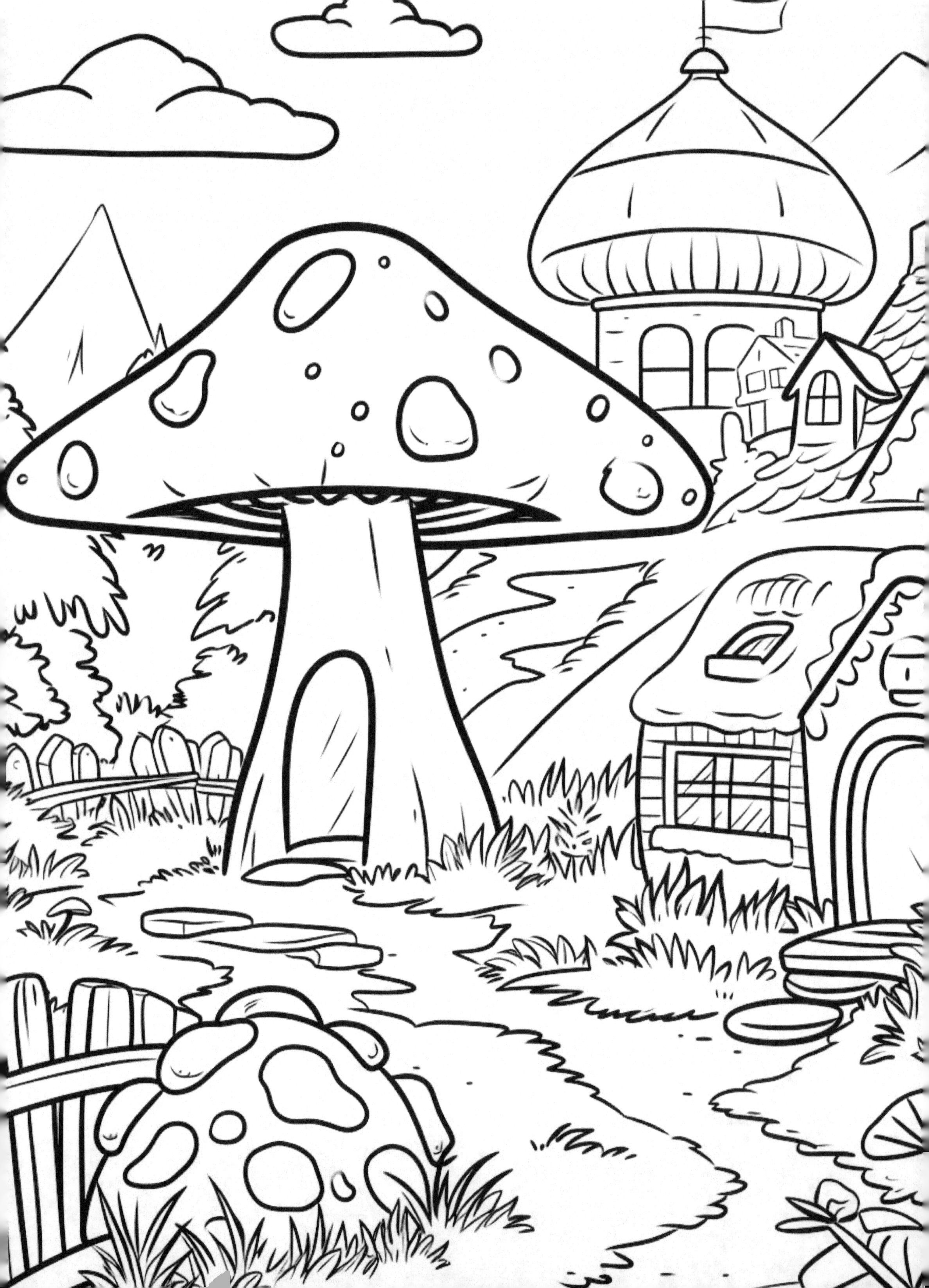

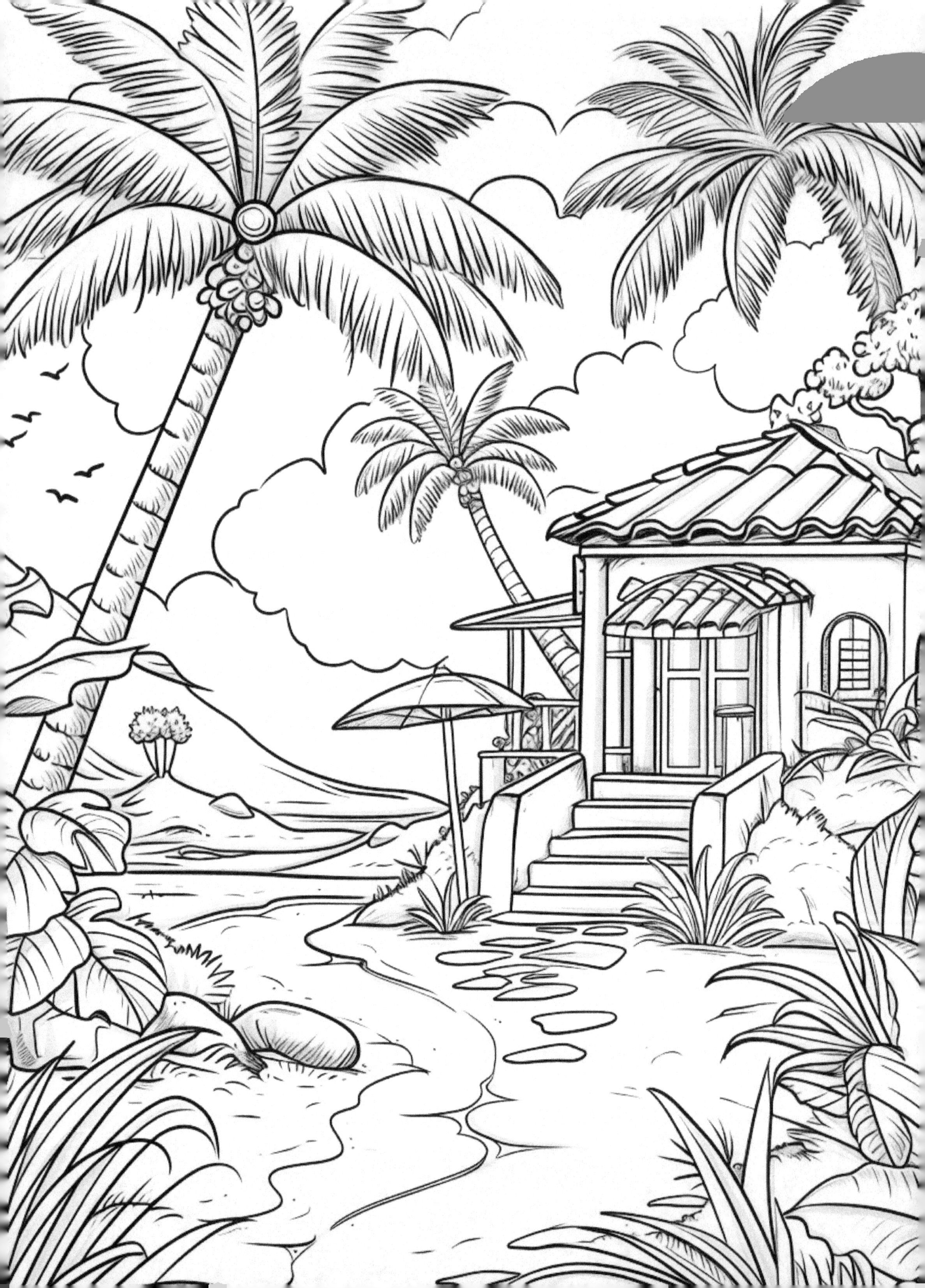

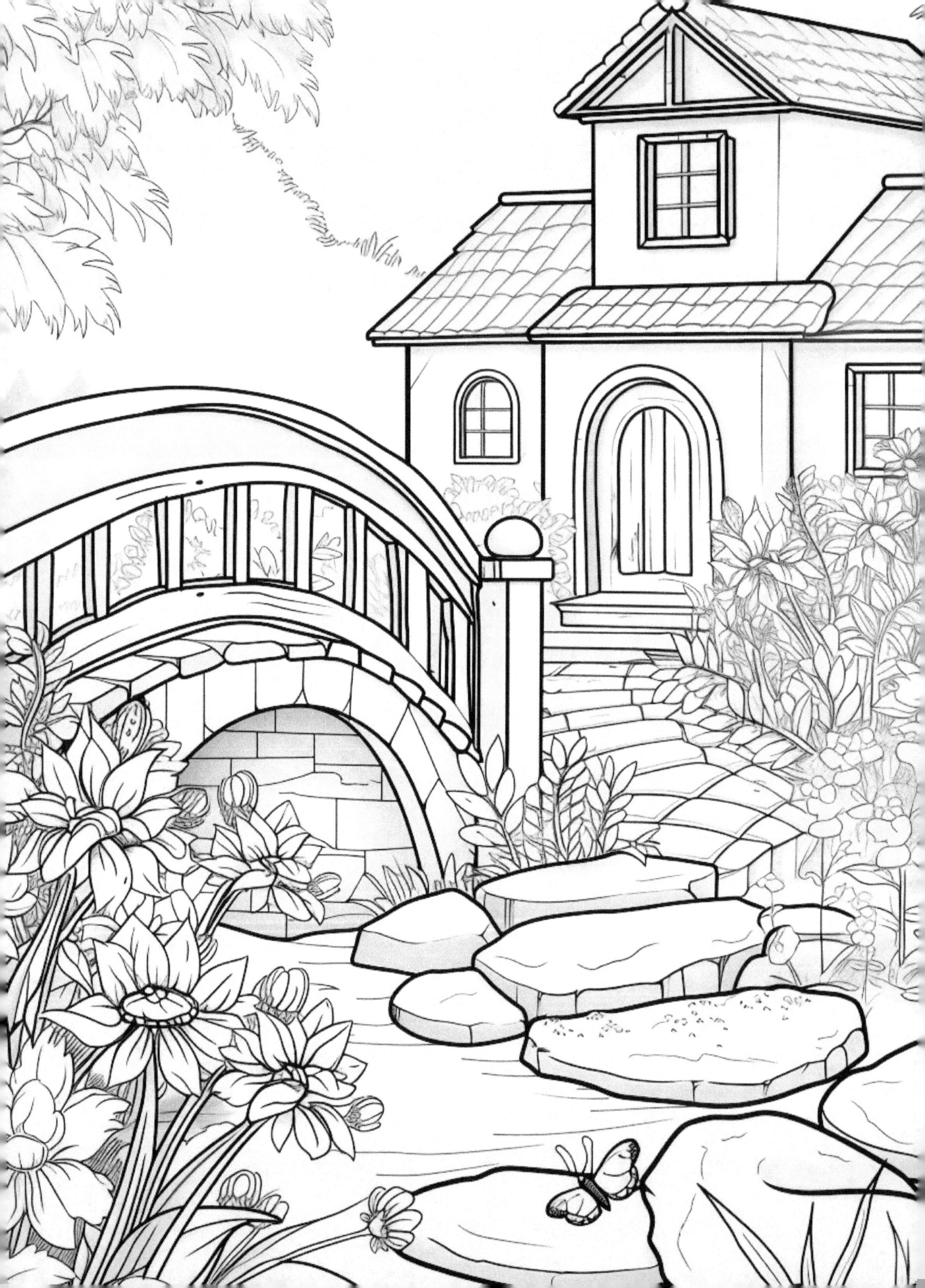

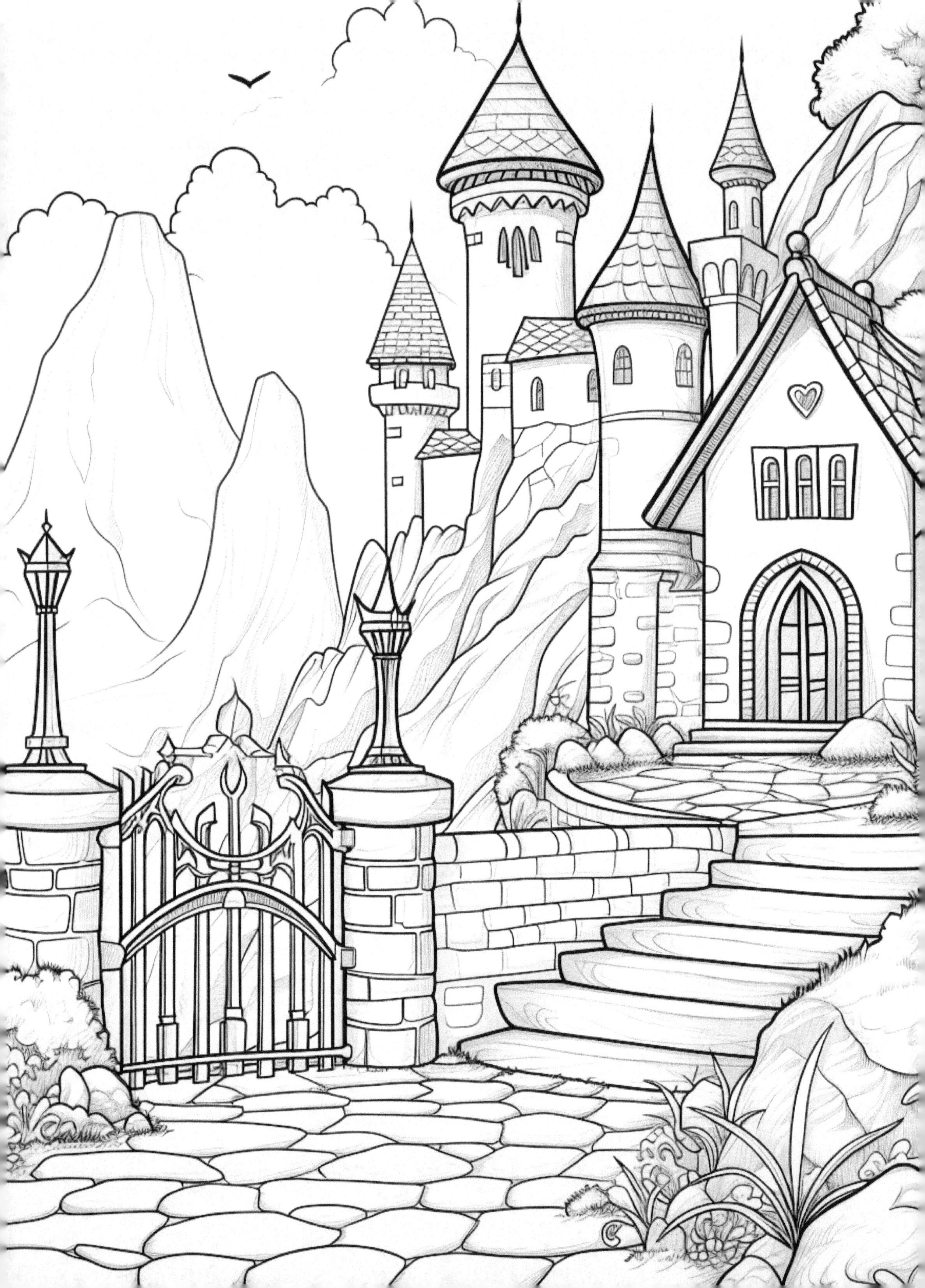

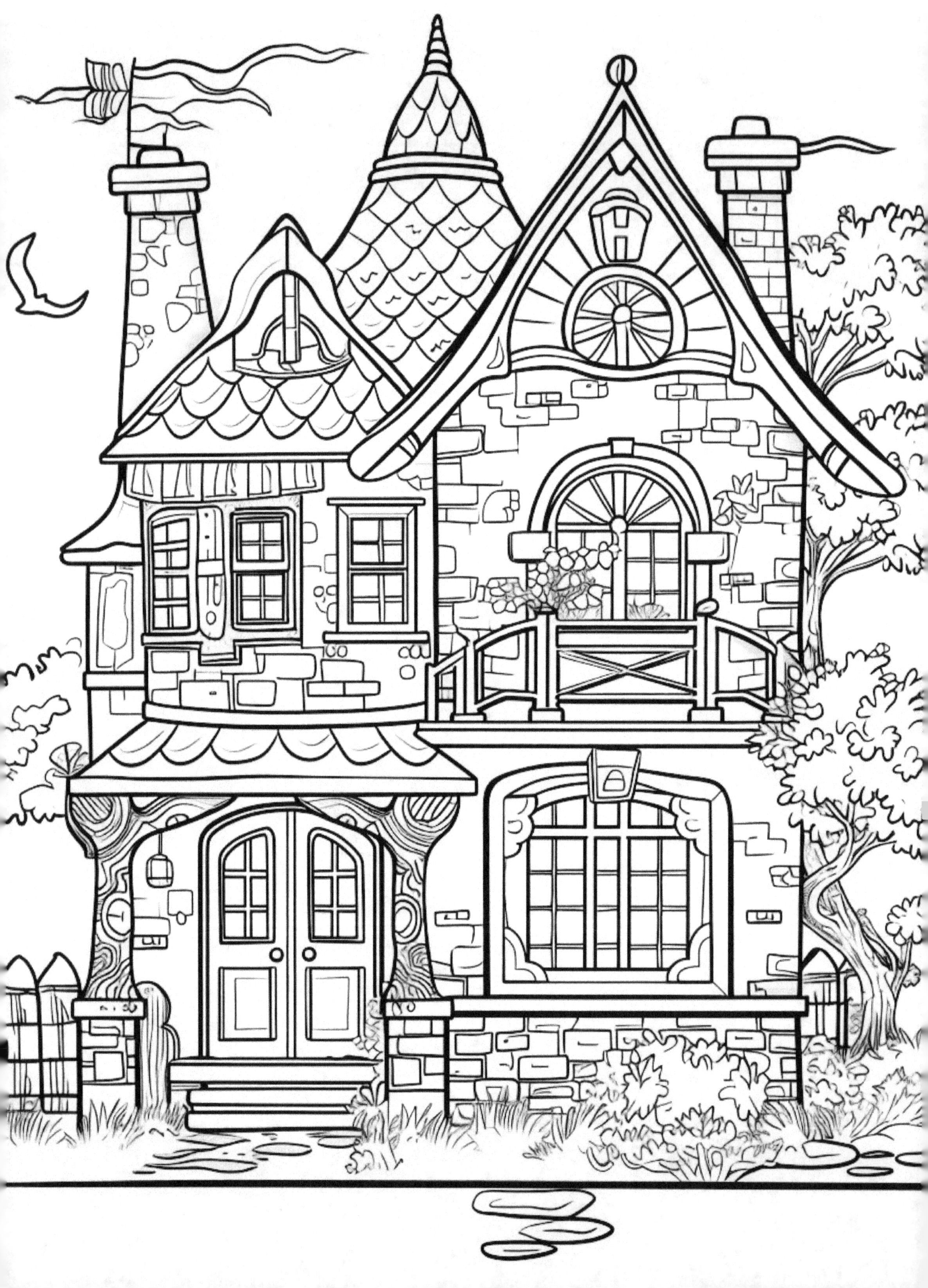

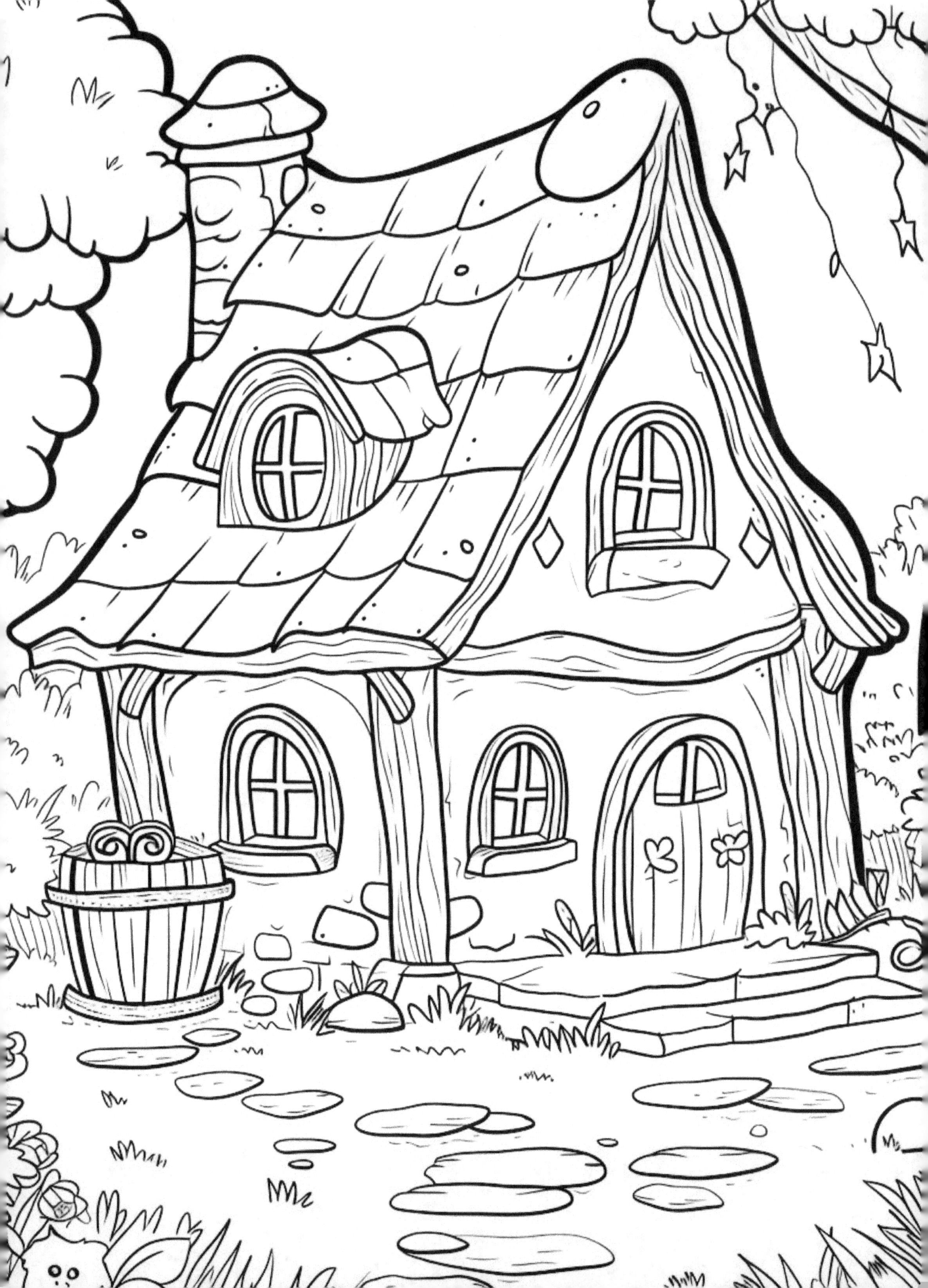

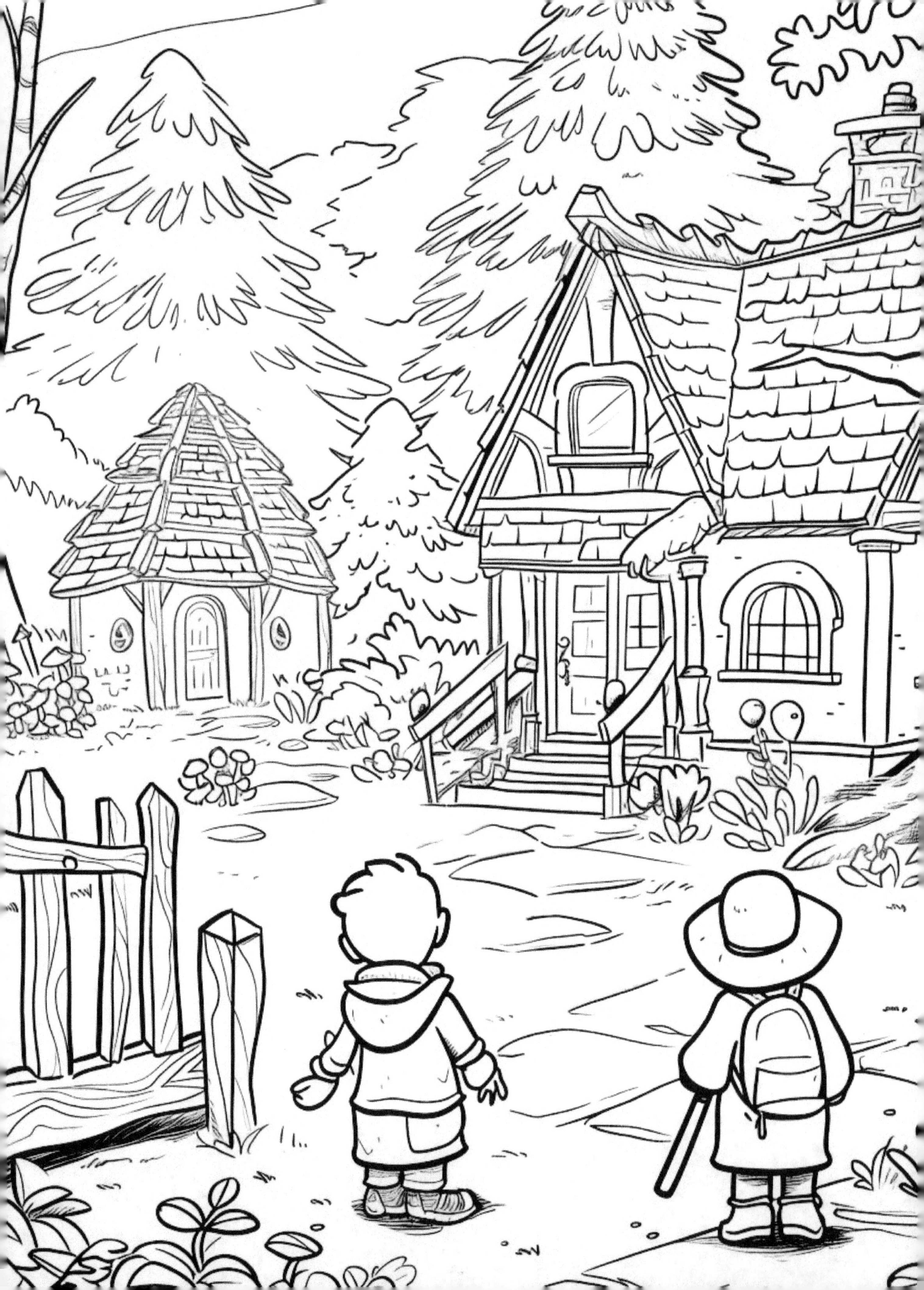

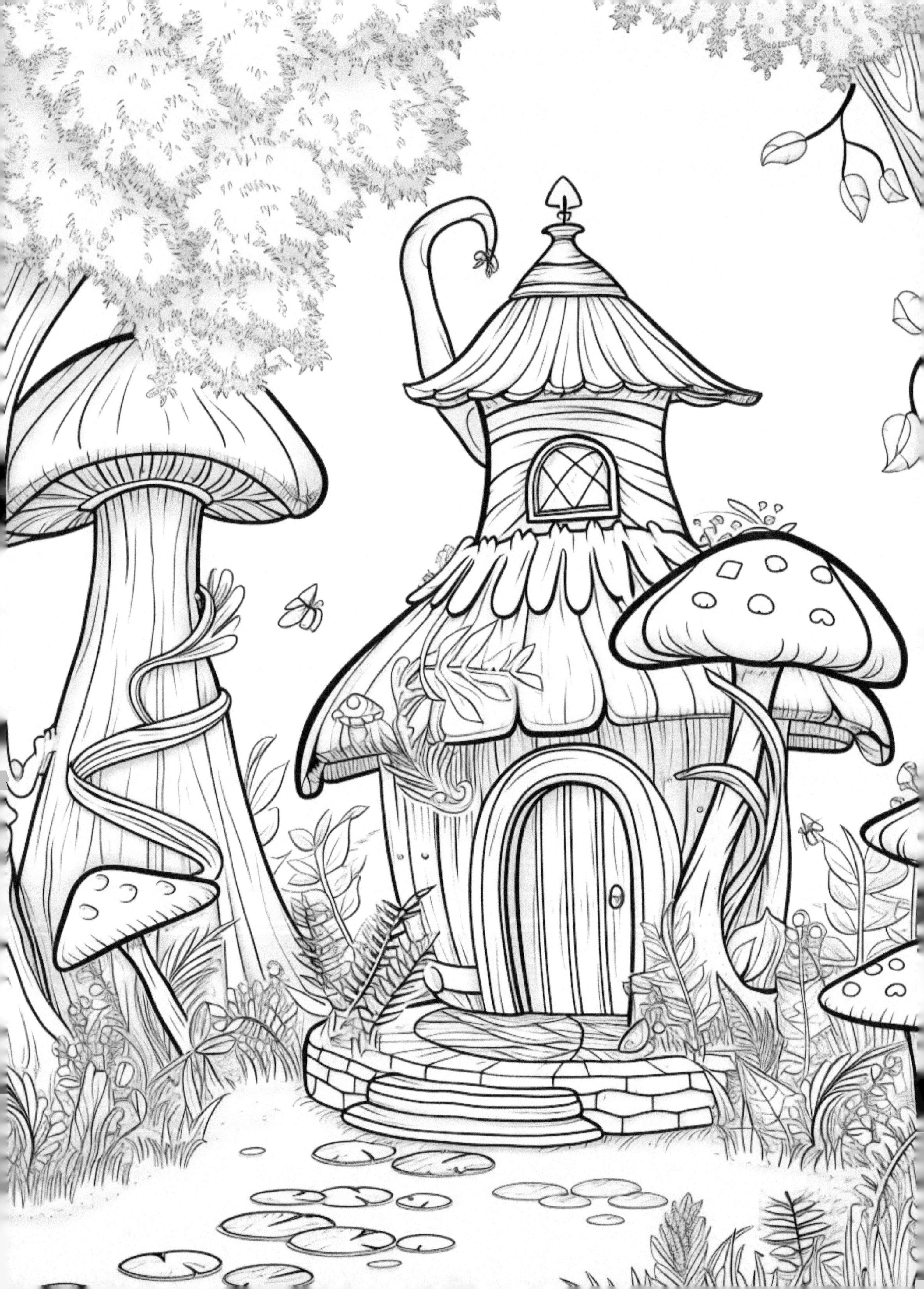

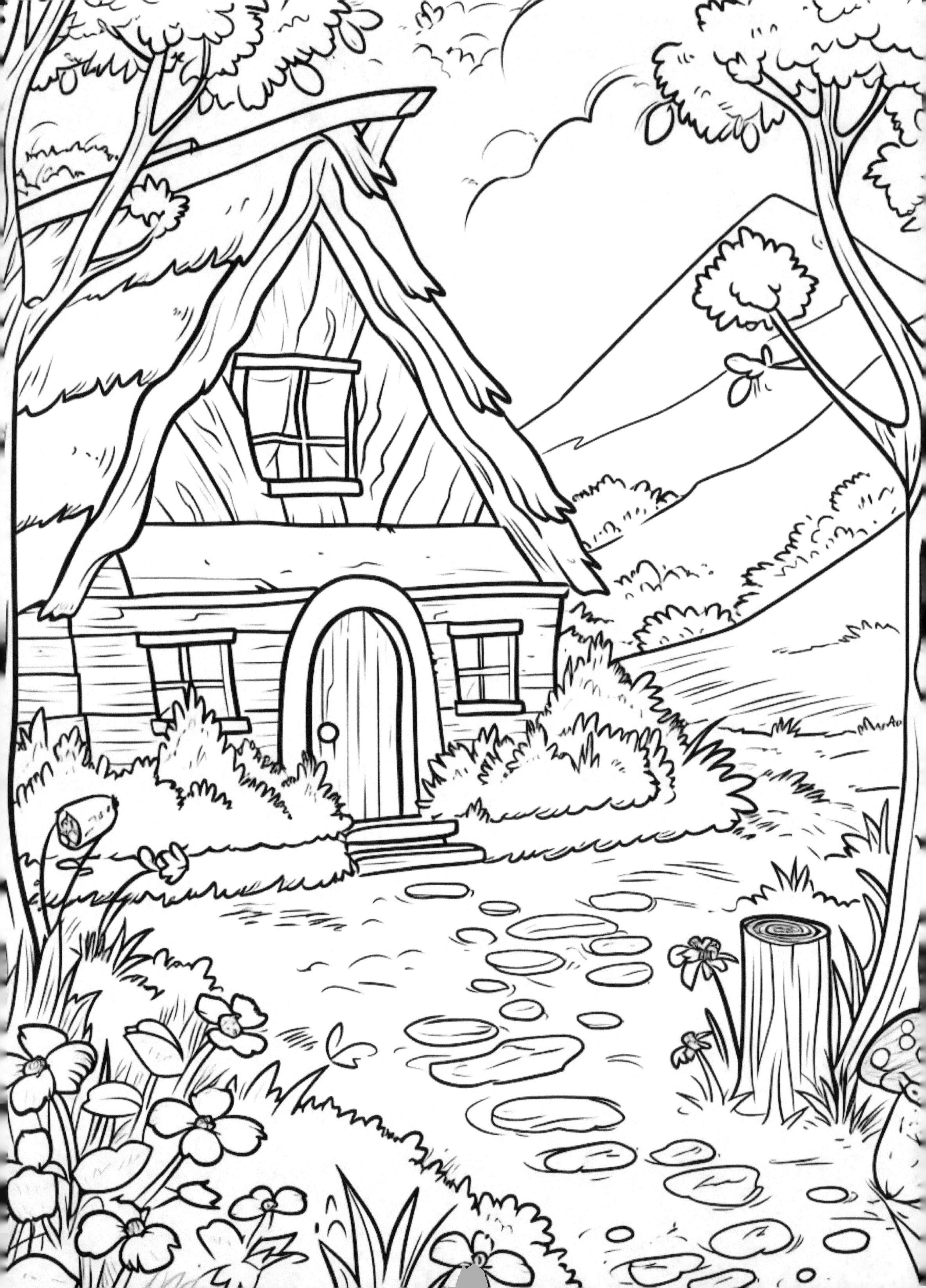

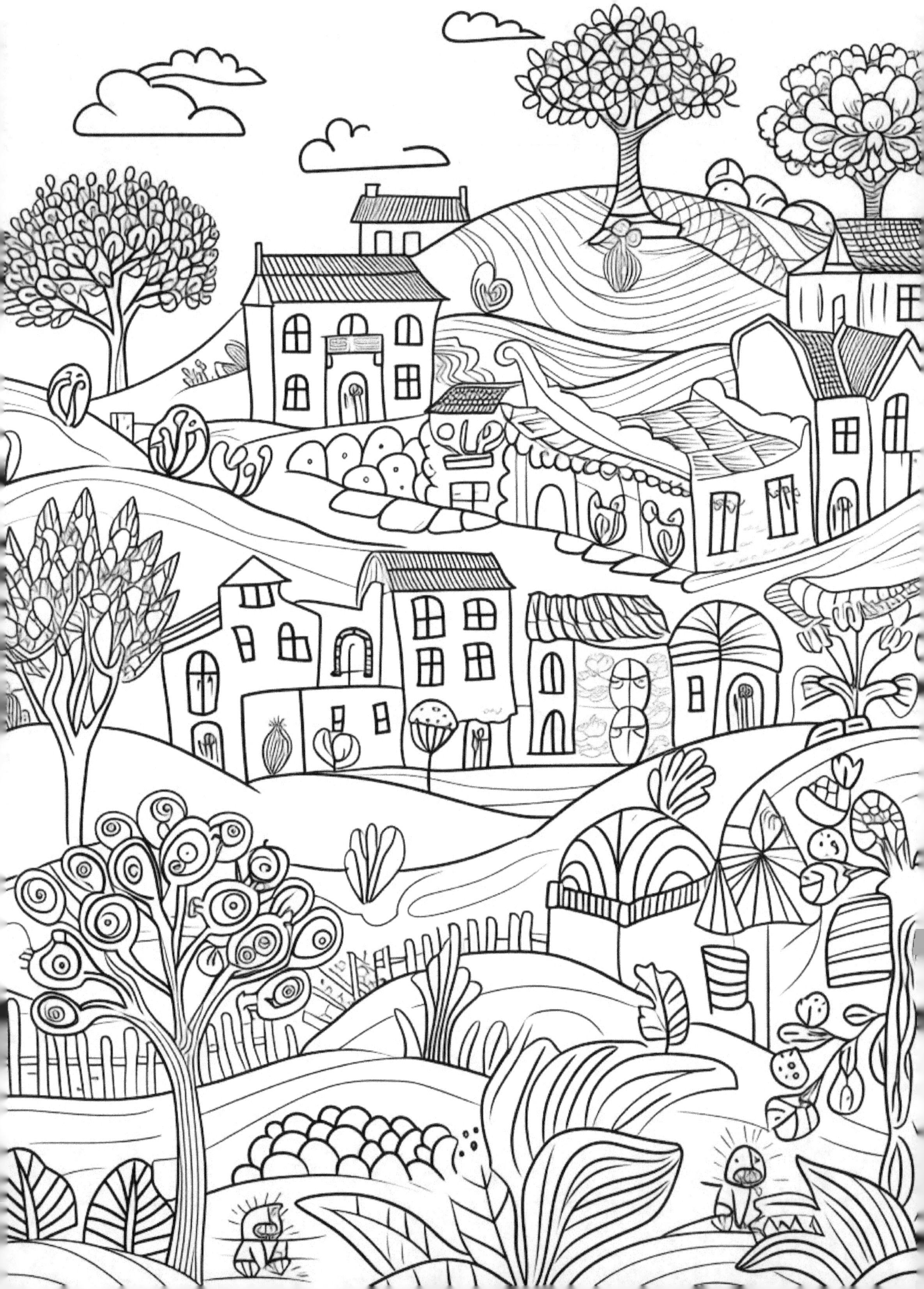

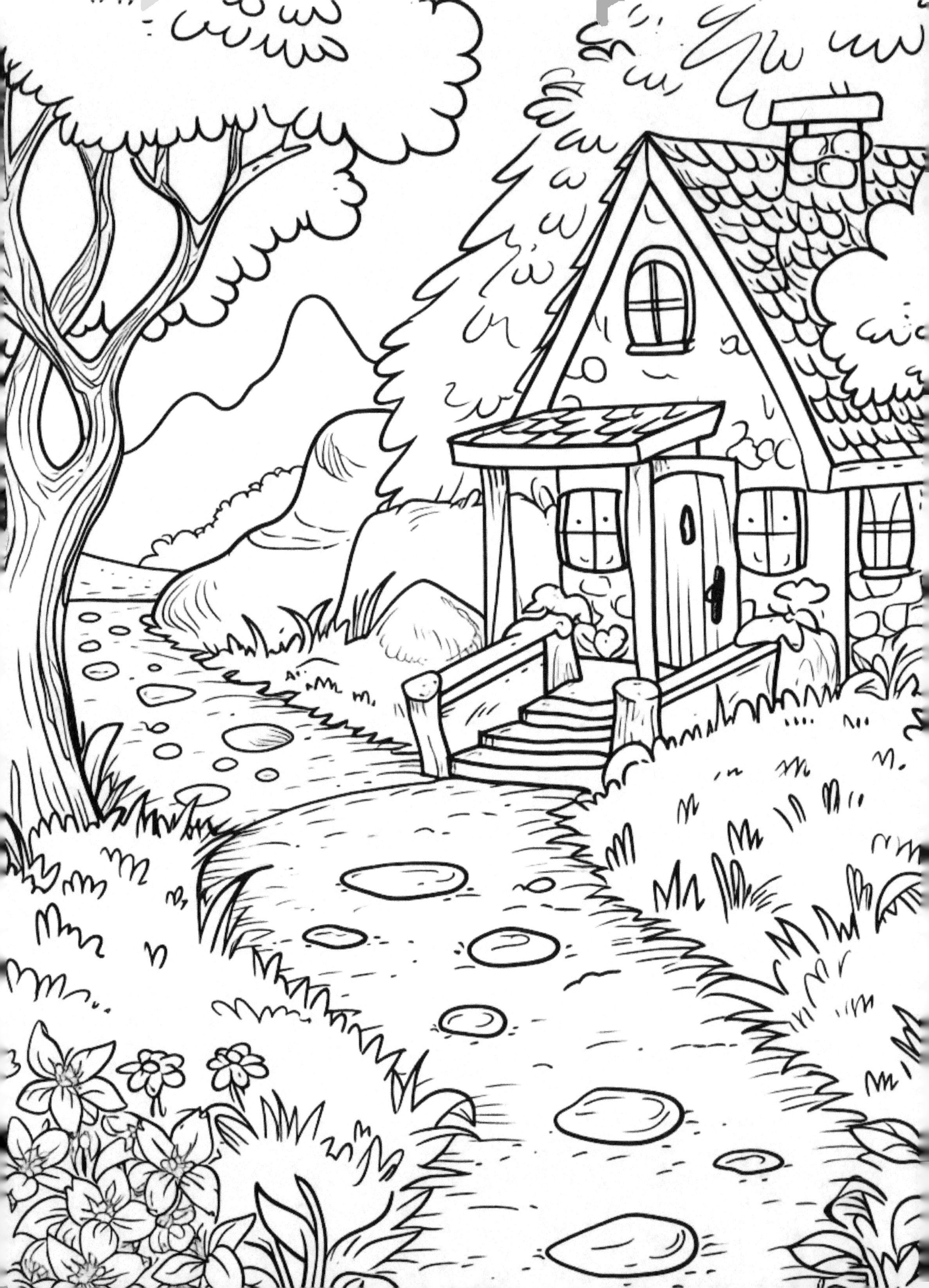

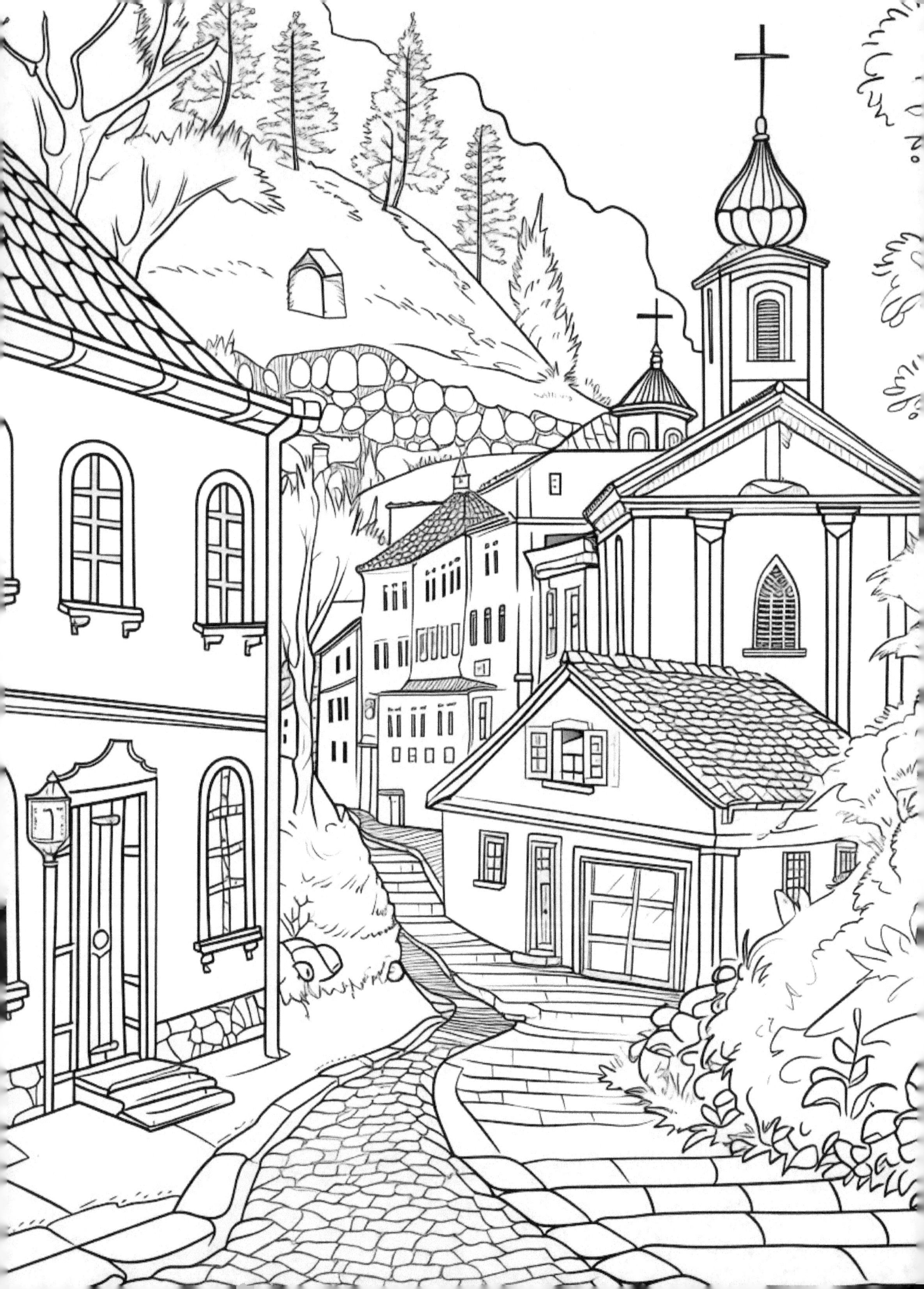

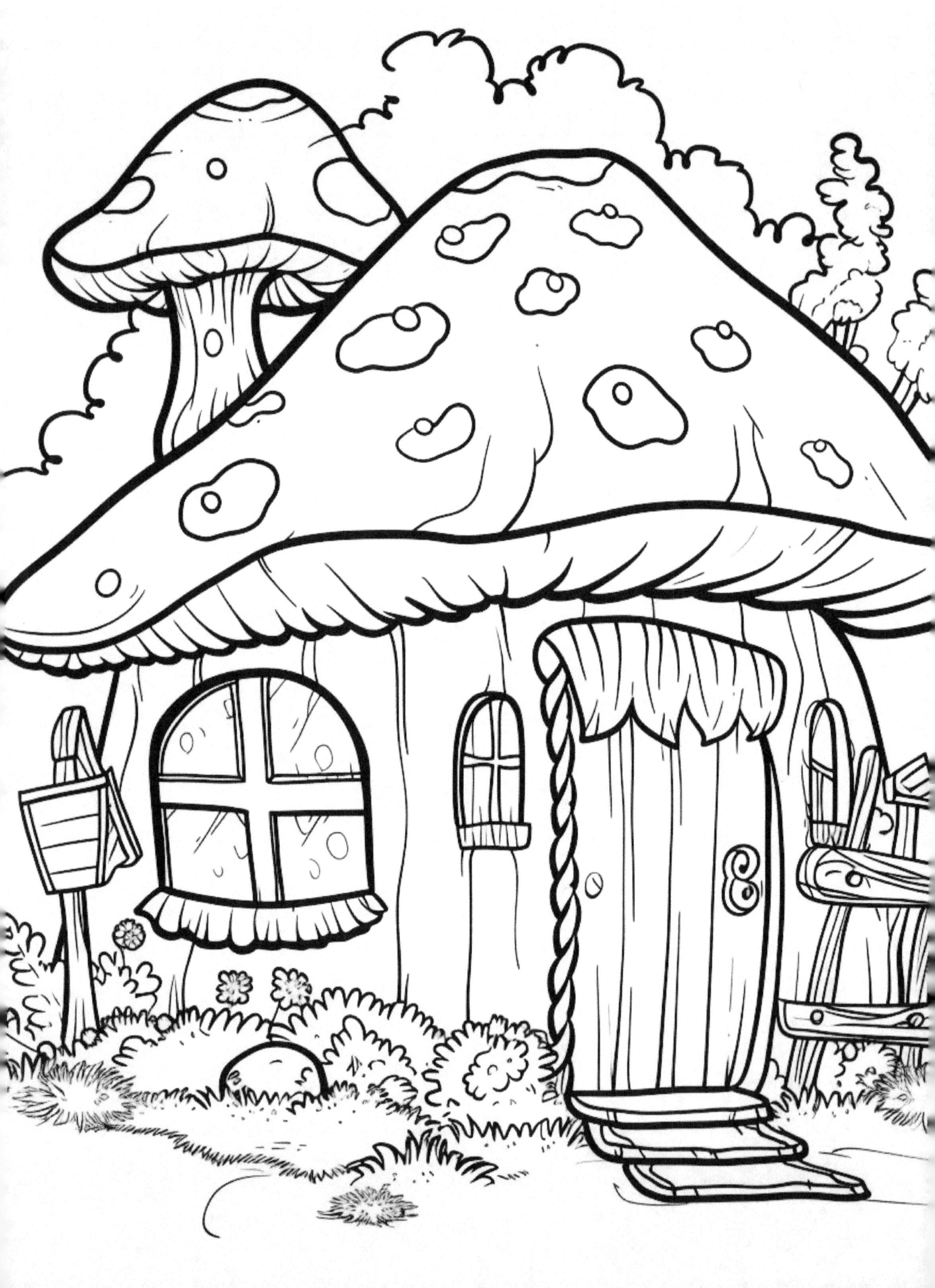

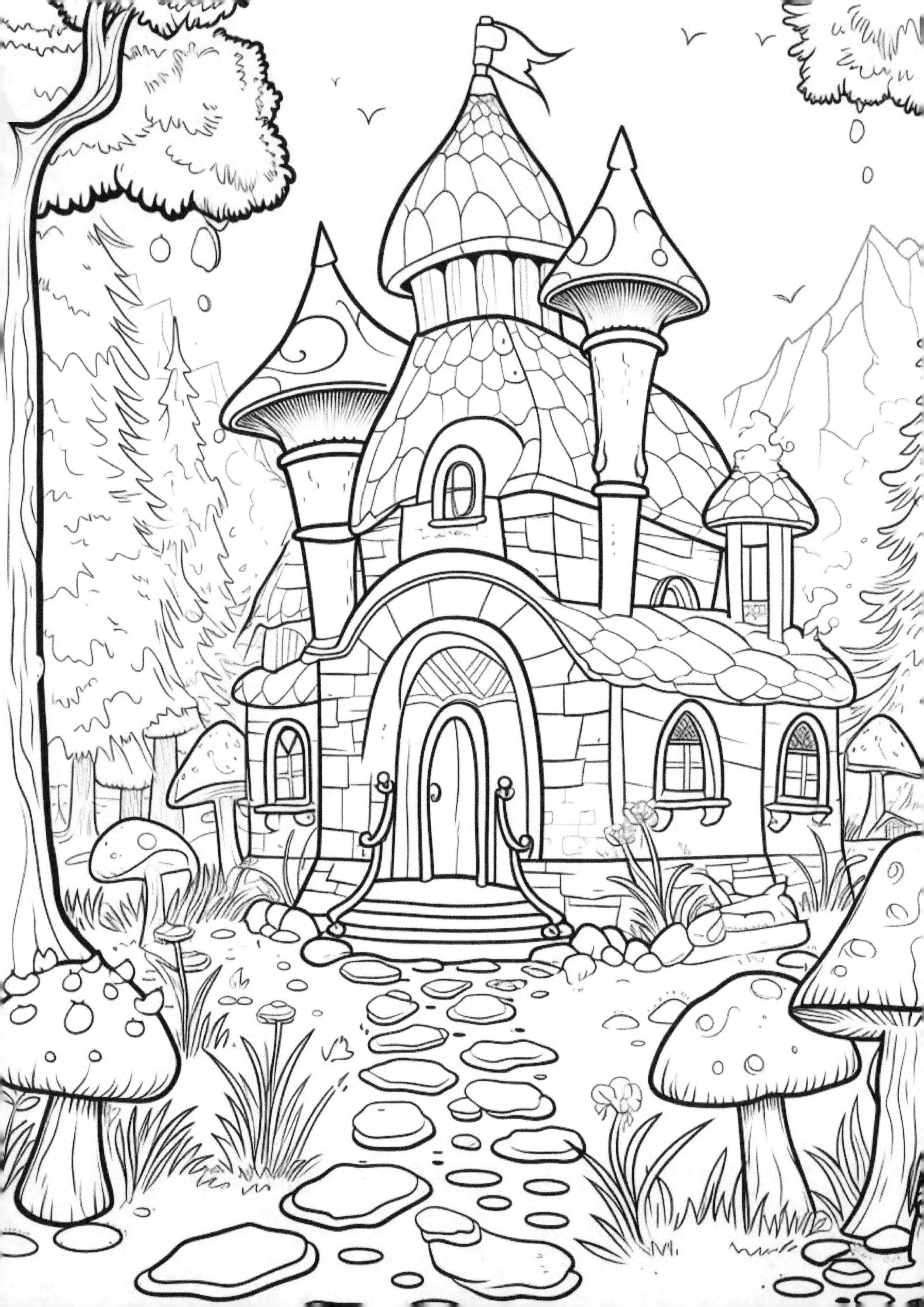

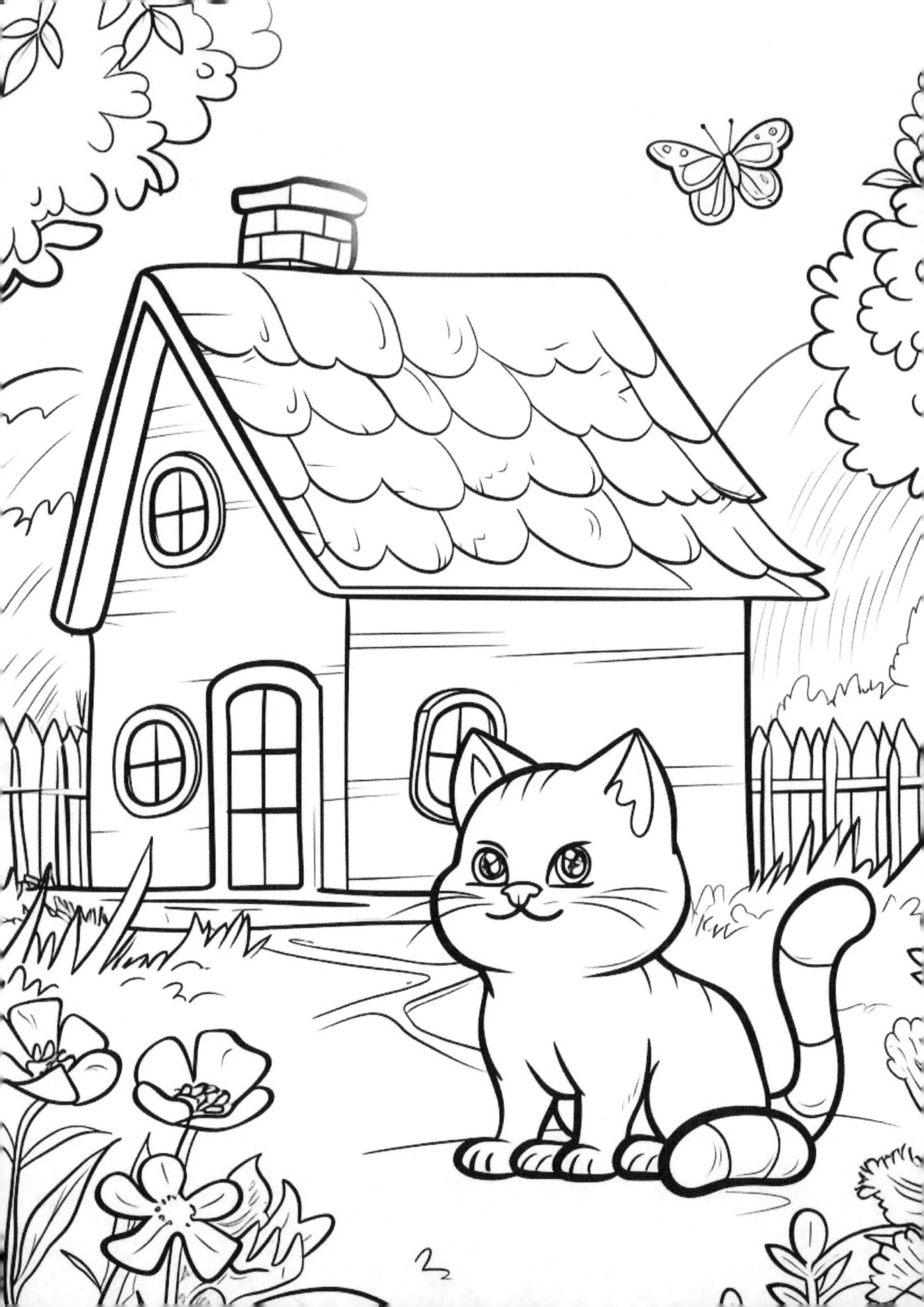

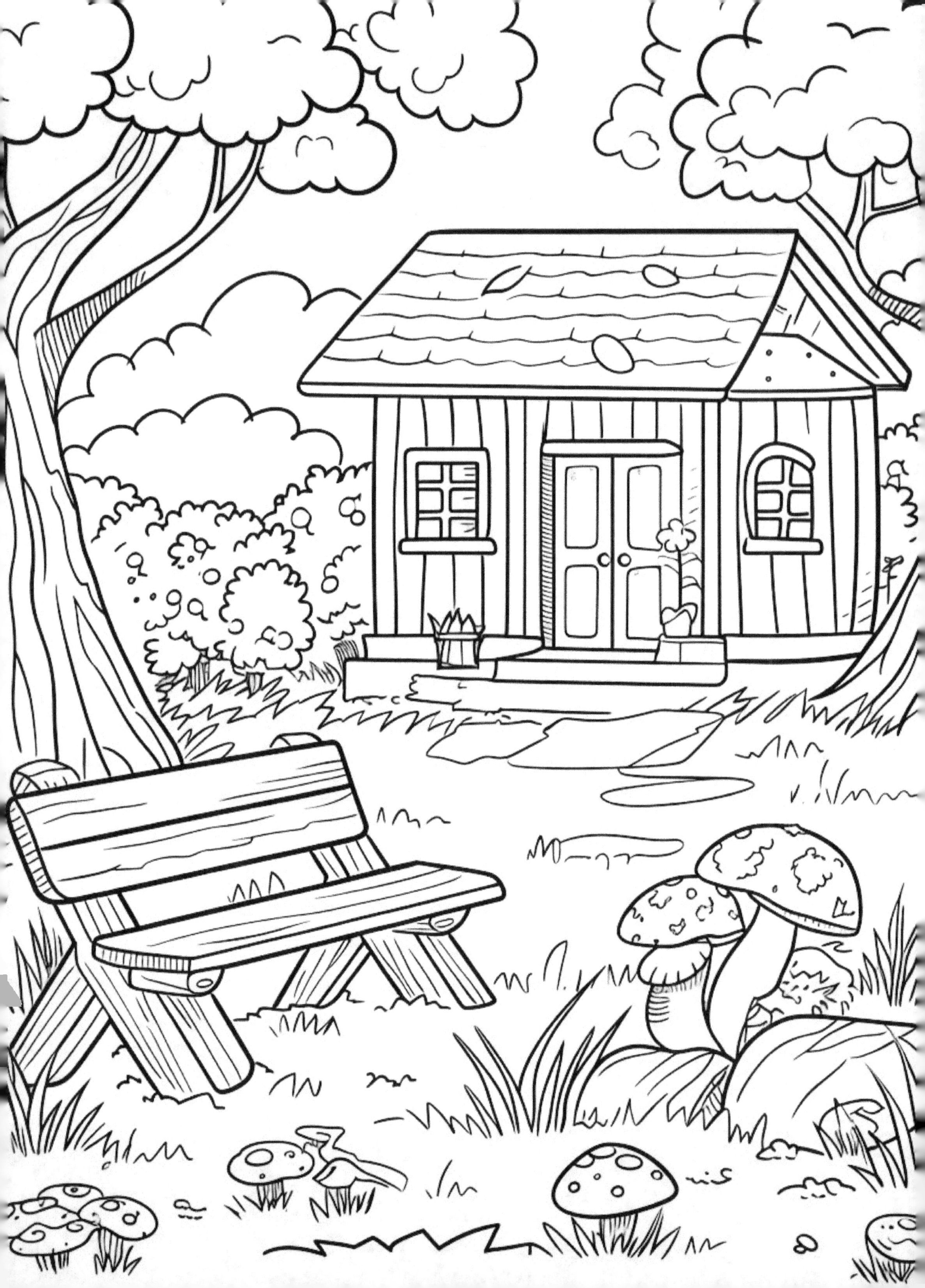

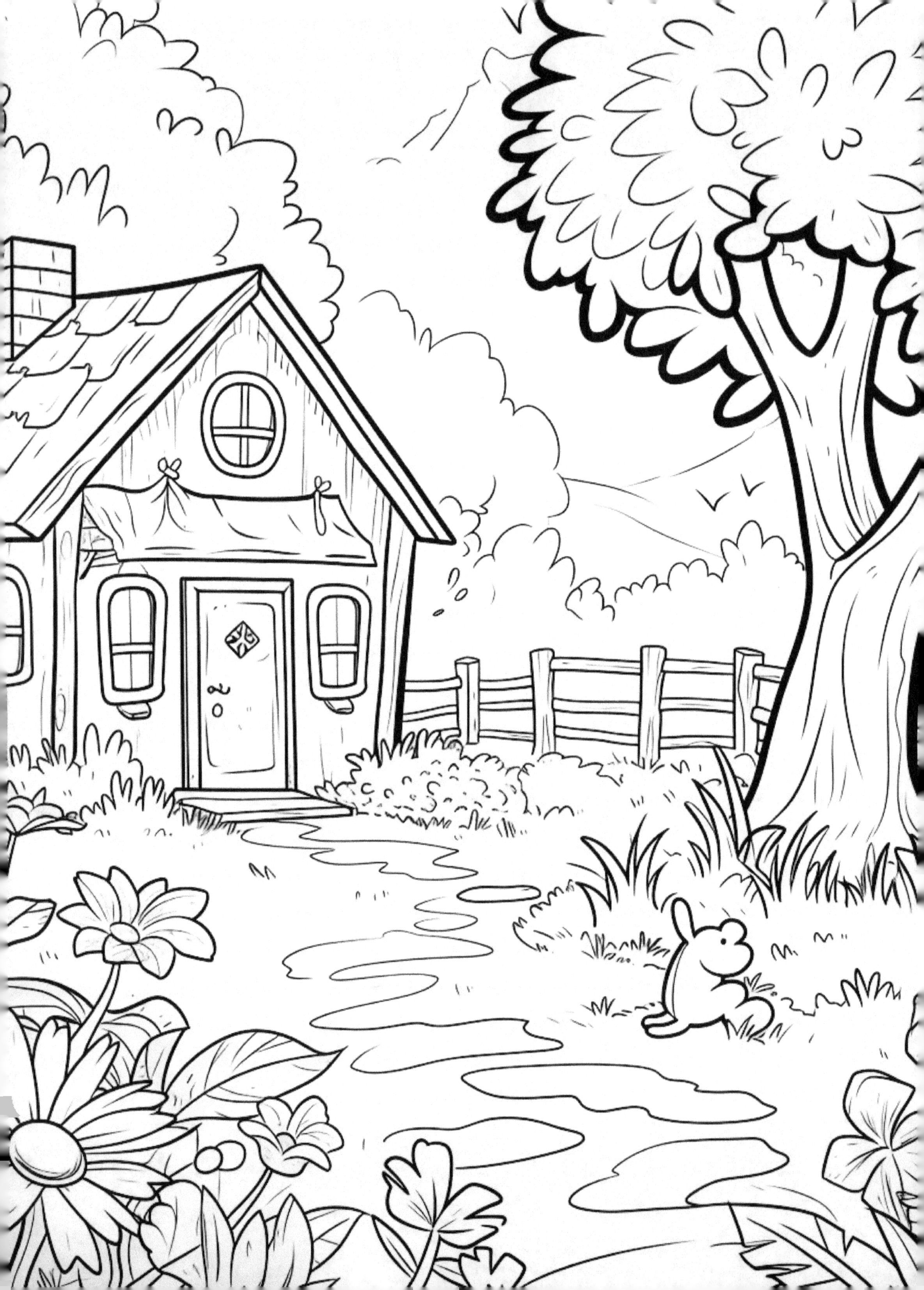

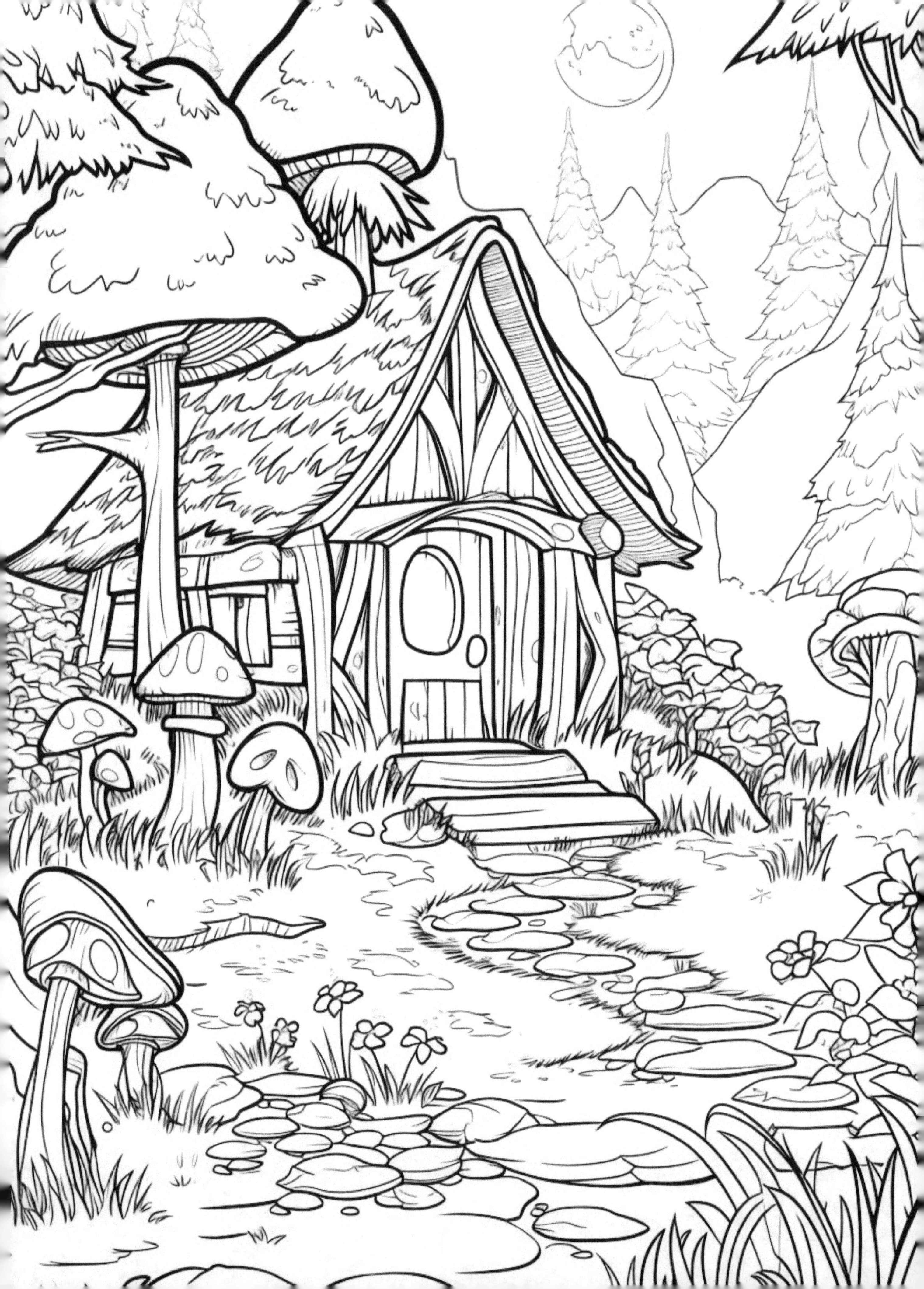

Thank you for joining me on this journey through 59 dream homes!

As you turn the final page, I hope your heart is filled with inspiration, your mind is sparked with creativity, and your soul is touched by the joy of coloring.

Remember, your dream home is not just bricks and mortar, but a canvas for your imagination. Keep coloring, keep dreaming, and keep creating!

With gratitude,
ARTUR SOBOLEVSKIJ